LEAVING THE PINK HOUSE

LEAVING
the
PINK HOUSE

⊷≔◉ ◖≕⊷

LADETTE RANDOLPH

UNIVERSITY OF IOWA PRESS
Iowa City

University of Iowa Press, Iowa City 52242

COPYRIGHT © 2014 BY LADETTE RANDOLPH

www.uiowapress.org
Printed in the United States of America

DESIGN BY TERESA W. WINGFIELD

The University of Iowa Press is a member of Green Press Initiative and is committed to preserving natural resources.

Printed on acid-free paper

Cataloging-in-Publication data on file with the Library of Congress

Work, love, build a house, and die.
But build a house.

—Donald Hall, *The One Day*

CONTENTS

LEAVING THE PINK HOUSE

September 2001

WE WEREN'T HOPEFUL that day in September as we headed south of Lincoln, Nebraska, on Highway 77 to look at what the ad had said was a "farmhouse on twenty acres fifteen miles from Lincoln." We couldn't help but notice as we drove, though, that instead of the usual suburban muck, the highway was lined by rolling hills, trees, well-tended farmsteads, and lovely vistas spreading out before us at the crest of each new hill.

I'd been doing this periodically—going to look at acreages—for the sake of my husband Noel. When he'd moved to Nebraska from San Francisco eleven years earlier, he'd fallen in love with the countryside in southeastern Nebraska, but he'd never particularly liked Lincoln. He preferred to live in either a large city or in the country. Not surprisingly, his dream since I'd met him had been to live in a house in the country. But at the time we married I'd protested. I wasn't going to put my grade-school children on a bus to attend a consolidated school. No matter what Noel felt about Lincoln, its public schools were among the most progressive in the state.

Despite this, in recent months I'd been humoring Noel with these occasional forays into the countryside. Indeed, my argument about the children's education was growing obsolete as the older two had already left home for college and the youngest was a junior at Lincoln High School. This was clearly something Noel wanted, and I, at times begrudgingly, admitted to myself it was his turn.

We'd seen property after property in various states of disrepair, or worse, old houses remodeled in "country" decor. Like many midwestern cities, Lincoln was developing irresponsibly, and almost every direction out of the city was lined with miles of development acreages, tract malls, and other evidence of sprawl. Our aversion to the unappealing drives and the inevitably disappointing properties on the other end had finally led Noel himself to conclude that owning a country house near Lincoln was probably impossible.

I BEST UNDERSTAND my life through the houses where I've lived. I have only to remember a particular house to summon clear memories of a given time and place. Like many adults, I've returned to those places—both in memory and in person—seeking from this exercise I'm not sure what: some part of myself, some time in the past I want to better understand. Houses are often the archives for my deepest, most resonant memories, the places where I've curated my life stories.

I was, however, slow to appreciate the value or pleasure in furnishing a home. In fact, when I was a young woman and had moved into my first house, I had no thought at all for creating a space that was both comfortable and beautiful. I simply didn't see things as *things* and couldn't make distinctions among them. At that time I cared only for what we needed: a few folding chairs and a stereo in the living room; in the bedroom, a twin bed (for two— my first husband and I were both very thin) and a small dresser; in the kitchen, a table and chairs. What more did we need? When visitors, not trying to hide their confusion, asked when the couch and chairs were coming, wondered where the TV was or why we hadn't hung any pictures, inquired politely how we slept together in that twin bed, I was honestly surprised. I hadn't considered we might need more.

When I was in my midtwenties, a friend opened my eyes to the world of things. Perhaps, like all such moments of recognition, it was a form of corruption, but it was also like seeing for the first time. This is the confession of an eccentric, of course. On that day in September, though, my former eccentricity, at least in this regard, was long in the past, and I now lived in a house full of antiques, wall hangings, rugs, dishes, and silverware. I was the owner and collector of things galore.

Here is another confession. The older I grow, the more terrified I become. Perhaps other people age toward wisdom, but with the years I have gathered only new fears. I am better able with time to imagine all the devastating ways a life can be altered. And with a family those fears are exponential. This isn't to say I'm fearful in my life. I've done a few bold things. Some of my past actions may even be called courageous. I've taken risks. I don't, however, actively seek excitement. I'm instead a devotee of the quotidian. At this time, I'm perhaps the happiest I've ever been in my life. I'm happy in my decade-long marriage to Noel. My three children are almost grown: Leif, twenty, and Jordan, eighteen (both students at the University of Nebraska), and Bronwyn, sixteen. I have meaningful work as an executive editor at the University of Nebraska Press. Noel is the operations manager for a grain elevator. We have good friends and supportive families. And I'm old enough—and perhaps this is wisdom after all—to know to treasure these as the most important of matters.

ONLY ONE THING was troubling me that day in September. My son Leif had recently announced his engagement to be married, a marriage that his entire extended family strongly felt was premature and misguided and that would most likely end in disaster. For the last few months I'd been preoccupied with Leif's situation and had found myself in a precarious position. I couldn't speak freely about my concerns, for it wasn't only Leif's future at stake in this marriage, but ours as well. As Noel had so grimly reminded me a few weeks earlier, "This woman may well be at our death beds." The dilemma of how to express apprehension for my son without offending him and his beloved had led me so far to silence.

I was in the midst of learning the hardest of lessons, that there's nothing more difficult to accept from our children than their repeating of our own mistakes. Precocious marriages had been encouraged by the religious milieu in which I was raised—and I'd paid a harsh penalty for leaving a youthful marriage. I wanted more than that for my children.

On the day of our drive out of town, we were living in a salmon pink house on Washington Street in the Near South neighborhood of Lincoln—an area just south of Lincoln's downtown and the University of Nebraska, within blocks of Nebraska's distinctive state capitol, fondly known as the penis of the plains. Like many urban neighborhoods, the western half of the Near South is densely populated, diverse, noisy with traffic. It's a mixed neighborhood in every sense, and for many people buying real estate in Lincoln it would be considered a risk. For every gentrified house in the neighborhood, another is falling into decline. Entire blocks of stately old homes have been brutalized into apartments, while in adjacent blocks houses have been lovingly restored. We had sought out property in that neighborhood knowing we wanted to live in as urban an environment as possible in Lincoln.

When Noel and I bought that house in 1992, it had been badly neglected for many years. We bought it intending to renovate. My three children from a previous marriage were grade-schoolers ages seven, nine, and eleven, and I was working and attending graduate school. Noel was commuting forty-five minutes both ways to work each day. We'd been married only the day before we moved in, and

I didn't yet know if Noel could actually do the renovations he'd promised. I'd known other men to make promises they couldn't keep. I remember looking at that mess of a house and at my new husband and deciding with grim resignation that I loved him immensely, and I was going to try to be happy there no matter what, that I would make it as much of a home as I could.

The house had good bones, though, and those structural features had shone through despite all its problems. What we had found on our first visit to the pink house with the realtors was a row of dark cedar trees glowering across the front of the porch, hiding it from the street. The exterior white paint was thick and buckled like an alligator's hide, the backyard a tangled mass of bushes, weeds, debris, and overgrown trees so tall the neighbors didn't know there was a two-story garage in the back. Inside, the interior walls had suffered water damage, and the plaster had cracked and peeled. Efforts to remodel the second story had been poorly conceived, though mercifully the oak woodwork on the main floor had not been painted over. The tiny, dark kitchen was like a closet in a cellar, the counters covered with the same peeling green linoleum found on the floor. We didn't even want to think about the basement. Although it was dry and the foundation sound, the previous owners had lived in the house since the 1930s and had built a hodgepodge of odd rooms, all of them filled with junk.

AS NOEL AND I had expected, given the low asking price, the farmhouse was in bad shape. Tall, persistent weeds and volunteer trees congested the north and the west sides of the house: sunflowers, ironweed, pigweed, ragweed, dock, thistle, mulberry saplings, and hedge apple saplings. The overgrowth was so thick and high we had to fight our way through to get to the outbuildings. When we reached them, we found only a weathered granary with a dirt floor in need of a roof and a wobbly pole barn surrounded by a six-foot-tall chain-link fence.

The best thing about the property was the broad lawn in front surrounded by old Siberian elms and locust trees. Four stately blue spruces bordered the gravel road across the front. The light was good, and the place felt like an old farmstead (which it was), rather than an acreage. The exterior of the house had been badly neglected but was certainly not the worst we'd seen. Avocado steel siding slipped off in places. An ancient roof curled at the edges and clearly needed to be replaced immediately. The door of the side porch sagged off its hinges, and the steps leading up to it were broken. Noel and I glanced at one another tentatively before entering.

The crow greeted us first. Confined inside the small porch, it screeched and threw its weight against the front of its four-by-four-foot cage, then settled back on its perch and straightened its feathers like a shrew smoothing her skirt after a tantrum. We took a step back as a woman with long blonde hair and a too-tight black dress opened the kitchen door. "Hi, I'm Angie, the realtor. Come on inside. Don't mind him. Ingrid, the woman who owns this place, rescues wild birds," she explained.

We were surprised to find Ingrid herself sitting at the kitchen table. Owners hadn't been present at previous open houses, and I was slightly uncomfortable with her there. Ingrid was a friendly woman, who would later tell us she had moved to Nebraska from Germany in 1970. She told us she had married a Lakota Sioux after she came to the U.S. They had since divorced, and her three sons were grown. She was moving to South Dakota to be nearer friends on the reservation. I couldn't guess her age. Her pale skin was unlined, and her blonde hair was as soft and fine as a child's.

Not only did the house stink inside, no doubt because of the numerous birds we soon found caged throughout, but the rooms felt cramped and dark. The small original house had been built sometime before the turn of the century and added on to in 1934, in the depths of the Depression, and again in the 1950s. It had most likely never had nice architectural features. Without looking too closely, we knew that the people who had built the original house and those who had built the additions had been pragmatic to the extreme and most likely would have cut corners whenever possible. The house's few windows were tall and narrow, letting in scant light. We found the usual suspects of 1970s remodeling: red, royal blue, and orange shag carpeting, dark wood paneling or faux brick on the walls, worn linoleum in the kitchen, and a narrow enclosed stairway leading to the second floor. We also noted the problem of the strange addition—two bedrooms and a bath with eight-foot ceilings (as opposed to the nine-foot ceilings elsewhere on the main floor). Noel quickly figured out the addition was resting on a concrete pad with no crawl space beneath it.

The air felt unhealthy, and I theorized that the sores I'd noticed covering Ingrid's arms and neck were caused by some kind of mites from the birds. My own skin itched thinking about it, and I struggled to breathe. In spite of all this, we found ourselves taking the house seriously.

"It's a gut job," Noel said under his breath at one point.

I nodded. "Could we take out the wall between the living room and dining room?"

Noel nodded thoughtfully. "I'd have to add a header if it's a supporting wall, but it could be done." After our first impression of feeling closed in, we realized the rooms were more generous than we'd initially thought. Still, the house was clearly smaller than the pink house and would never, despite any expense and effort, be as grand. Nothing was salvageable except for the wood floors we assumed were under the carpets. We had to think of it in terms of space only.

"We could move the entrance," I tentatively suggested. "Open it into the living room instead of the kitchen."

Noel nodded.

On some level I couldn't believe we were having this conversation. I had no intention of leaving the life I loved in the pink house, yet I seemed to be caught up in the temporary vision of rebuilding this sad old place. Not because I believed at that time it could ever be beautiful, but because the view to the east of an old red barn and a windmill in a rolling meadow flanked by trees was so peaceful and familiar I could almost imagine living there.

As the afternoon drew to a close, I sat outside at a picnic table with Ingrid and Angie while Noel nosed around the foundation. Now and then he came around with a question. "So, your sewage is handled by a lagoon system?"

"How deep is the well?"

"That water's been tested?"

When he wasn't there, the three of us talked about the birds Ingrid had observed on the property through the years. That's when she told me about the two half-wolf dogs she'd kept penned inside the six-foot fence around the pole barn. She had to put them down, the hardest thing she'd had to do, because she couldn't take them with her to South Dakota. The house she'd bought there was in town. She explained how she reinforced the fence around the pole barn with rebar because the dogs would get out and fight with the coyotes. I thought then of our wheaten terrier, Finnegan, who looked very much like a little sheep. I didn't figure he'd be able to hold his own against coyotes. I looked off to the south end of the property, dense with trees and tall grass, and imagined coyotes watching us.

"Are you hunters?" Ingrid asked. "Would you plan to hunt?"

"No," I said. "We aren't into that."

Despite my earlier envisioning of renovations, I was confident we wouldn't be taking on this project, and I answered Ingrid's questions with nonchalance. Still, we were the last to leave the open house. Other prospective buyers had come and gone, all with similar looks of disgust. I'd heard comments as we'd gone from room to room inside. In the basement, I overheard one disgruntled man say to his wife, "Why can't the whole place look like this?" He was referring to the new foundation under part of the house. A new furnace and air conditioner sat against the east wall. The concrete floor was swept clean. Bird feed sat tidily in forty-pound bags on wooden pallets. In the end, it was that solid basement Noel used to convince me to call Jan and Terry Gaber when we got back home that night. They were the realtors who'd sold us the pink house.

Jan and Terry had worked for Woods Brothers for many years. Terry, pink-cheeked and balding, with clear blue eyes, seemed to take a backseat to Jan when they were together. She'd been a surgical nurse earlier in her life, and that focused efficiency still characterized her. Terry had started painting landscapes recently, and we sensed he wanted to retire. Over the years Noel had called Terry now and then to go look at acreages, but we hadn't seen Jan since we bought the pink house. More importantly, they hadn't seen the house since they sold it to us. We could still remember the pained expressions on their faces nine years earlier as we walked together through room after dismal room of it. It had been clear they thought we were making a mistake to buy the place.

They, too, remembered its original state and were impressed with the work we'd done in the years since. "You'll have no trouble selling," Jan said, while Terry nodded cheerfully. They loved especially the kitchen with its large multipaned windows overlooking the secluded backyard garden and patio.

"It's best to sell in the spring," Jan said.

"But sometimes a Christmas house can sell well," Terry added. "This house would show beautifully at Christmas."

"The problem is," Noel explained, "the place we're interested in is another fixer-upper. A *major* fixer-upper. We couldn't live there while we did the work."

They drove out to the property with us the next afternoon to let us take a second look. If they had doubts, they didn't let them show as they walked calmly through the house. Finally Jan delivered this verdict. "After seeing what you've done with your current house, you'll make this into a showplace in no time." I wanted to share her certainty but was in fact horrified things had gone this far. I couldn't imagine why I was so passively going along when I clearly didn't want to leave my home. That was September 10th.

Then came September 11th, and everything changed. My confusion deepened. Besides being risky, it felt frivolous, even decadent to be thinking about buying another house after such a traumatic event. Across the country on that day, there was an overwhelming fear that life as we'd known it would change for the worse. Would banks collapse? Would the economy dry up? Would we have jobs? And in tandem with all these fears I found myself making a corresponding set of propositions: At the new house, we would have our own well. Twenty acres would be enough to raise food to live on. We'd be away from the city. There'd be room for our families if need be. These strange survivalist thoughts surprised me, but in the wake of the attacks on the World Trade Center, thinking logically was perhaps not anyone's first concern. And yet, what *were* we thinking? Left to ourselves, we would have done nothing. Left to ourselves, we would have sunk into lethargy. At the very least we would have waited. But we weren't left to ourselves. We had an appointment to meet with Jan and Terry the next day. We kept our appointment.

In the days following September 11th, everyone in the country seemed to be in a fog of shock and grief. We were all grappling with a new sense of our own vulnerability, and no one had answers. Despite this, business went on as usual. And so it was that on the 12th of September, after another tour of the country house, I found myself sitting beside Noel in the backseat of Jan and Terry's car seriously discussing an offer on the property, as the autumn sky grew dark around us. The reason for the hurry was the threat of two other offers. The low asking price had attracted other buyers capable of such major renovations, and Ingrid had already turned down one offer because she didn't like the people.

Before we made an offer, though, I wanted to meet the neighbors. A common bane in rural Nebraska at that time were farmhouses turned into meth-labs. We risked being rude that night as at 9:30 we knocked on the door of the house three hundred yards down the gravel road, the property in our lovely view to the east. The windows were dark, but cars were parked out front. It took a few minutes before anyone answered, while inside several dogs barked furiously.

As soon as they answered the door, we knew Mark and Linda Gentleman were all right. They were friendly, open, and polite enough to reassure us we weren't bothering them, even though we later learned Mark typically left for work by 5:30 A.M. and was probably already in bed when we knocked. Mark was stocky and handsome, his dark hair trimmed close and his black goatee tidy. He looked a bit like a young Burt Reynolds. Linda, blonde, pretty, and vivacious, introduced their two corgis, Shadow and Augie, and their German shorthair, Mason.

Noel explained we were interested in the property across the road and went on to ask, "Do you know if there are any plans for a bypass through here? A toxic waste dump? A maximum security prison? Anything we should know about?" Later, we wondered why we hadn't called the Lancaster County Planning Commission earlier that day to get more accurate information about the county's plans for this area, but the Gentlemans assured us that night that they hadn't heard of anything suspicious happening in the area. As it turned out, they had bought their ten acres only a couple of years earlier. Without our asking, they told us they planned to maintain the red barn and the meadow where it sat.

Forty-five minutes later, as we trudged back up the gravel road where the Gabers were patiently waiting, we decided to make an offer.

"Is it too late to be doing this?" Noel asked, noting that it was after 10:00.

"No," Jan said. Inside the house Ingrid waited with Angie and a friend. We offered what we felt was a reasonable price given the work we'd have to do, and after an hour of fairly innocuous nego-tiations, Ingrid accepted our offer.

"Ingrid hoped you'd buy the place," Angie later admitted. "She liked you that day of the open house."

Ingrid clarified this: "I know you won't let anyone hurt the birds here." It was very late by the time we signed the necessary papers and wrote the check for the earnest deposit, and we were exhausted as we got into our car to begin the half-hour drive home. For several miles we drove in stunned silence. What had we just done? What had we been thinking? When we finally began to talk and to express our fears about what felt like a rash decision, Noel, who is an emotional man, said in a voice near tears, "Have I done damage to our relationship by pushing this thing?" I didn't know how to answer him. I felt simultaneously numb and terror stricken. I loved Noel for being the kind of man who was sensitive enough to know such things can cause damage in relationships, but a squeeze of his hand was the extent of my reassurance.

He went on then, "It's not the new place that's bothering me, it's saying goodbye to the old house." I wasn't nearly at that point yet. I was already panicked about the logistics of selling that house we loved, and packing, and moving. When would we have to move?

And more importantly, what would we move into? These pragmatic worries kept me from feeling sentimental. Instead, I felt as
though my world had suddenly turned upside down, and there
was no one to blame for the upheaval but myself. I still couldn't
figure out why I'd let things go so far. Noel had fantasized like
this before without my becoming an accomplice. But this time had
been different, and I couldn't understand why, except for what had
happened the day before in New York. Otherwise, the entire trans-
action befuddled me. It was completely out of character for me not
to have considered these questions before making an offer. And
it was in the midst of my very real concerns that I remembered
something. "Didn't Terry mention tonight some kind of loan we
can get to fix up the house before having to move?"

Noel nodded. "A bridge loan."

"He said six or nine months, right?"

Noel nodded again, and I felt my panic begin to subside. "I've
been thinking," Noel said. "What about this? We take out a bridge
loan for nine months and start working on this house."

"If," I added, "during construction we decide we don't feel good
about it, we'll sell this place and stay in the pink house." We both
felt relieved by this prospect, and it liberated us to begin talking
about what we would need to do first.

That night as we drove, we started a preliminary plan for how
we'd proceed. Already, we felt the clock ticking. First the roof, we
decided, and we wouldn't try to do it ourselves. There wouldn't
be time. As it was, it would be a race against the weather, and
depending on the closing date, we might risk rain or snow causing the shingles not to seal. Before they began to roof, Noel would
need to tear down the two old chimneys to below the roofline. He'd
tear off the side porch and build another entrance, and he'd start
demolishing. Everything, except the exterior shell, the frame, the
basement, and the floors, would go.

When we told the kids about our decision the next day, their reactions were typical of each of their personalities. Leif, laid-back and dreamy, merely said, "Cool." Jordan, by nature conservative and a seasoned worrier, said, "Are you crazy?" While Bronwyn, who craved change and was always ready for an adventure, said, "When are we moving!"

We decided against telling our neighbors until we knew for certain whether we'd move or not, but the reactions of friends and family ran the gamut from "How wonderful. I've always wanted to live in the country" to "How can you think of leaving your beautiful home?" My own feelings vacillated hourly: one minute caught up in the urgency of planning, the next devastated by how this decision would change my contented life. I kept hoping something would happen or someone would say something to help resolve the question for me, but no such moment came.

One thing I did decide in those first days was that this was chiefly Noel's project, and although I'd help as much as I could, he couldn't assume I'd be free to go along with him to work on the house every night and every weekend. I had a demanding job and one kid still at home, and I didn't want my labor to be taken for granted. As it was, I knew already my energies would be consumed in making decisions about more details than I wanted to imagine. Suddenly, there were so many things, so many choices about those things, and all the decisions would need to be made quickly. I may not be as eccentric as I once was about material things, but I can still get overwhelmed by such decisions. Frankly, I would always rather be reading a book. All I could see before me now were the endless details that would demand my time and attention in the months ahead and the ways they would distract and consume me. The dream was still not mine, and I knew I'd resent it if I were expected to simply subordinate all my own energies to it.

Noel, who respected my feelings, nonetheless wanted me to see how this project would change him after we took possession of the house. "You have to understand, for the next nine months this house is going to be my life," he said. I did see that, and I missed him already.

THE DAYS FOLLOWING the offer included a visit to the bank. With Jan and Terry's recommendation, our own good credit, and the pink house as collateral, we had no trouble getting a nine-month bridge loan for the purchase price plus additional funds toward the first costs of renovation. The closing date was set for October 29th. As soon as we left the bank, we felt the pressure of how short a time we had in which to complete the monumental work ahead before the requisite inspection at the end of the loan period. Once we began demolition, the country house would lose its value immediately, and we'd be the owners of a nearly worthless construction site. At the end of nine months, we'd have to satisfy the bank's inspector that not only was the house worth at least the purchase price but that it now met other safety codes as well. Never mind that most of those codes hadn't been met at the time of purchase. It was the bank's regulation, and we had to comply. We couldn't allow ourselves to worry about what might happen to interest rates during the volatile time post-9/11 when, at the end of the bridge loan on July 29th, we would lock in to our permanent loan. We'd ventured into the unknown, and we'd have to deal with the challenges as they came. There was no way to completely anticipate or prepare for what we'd find when we began to tear down and rebuild that old house.

As we looked at the list of things we needed to begin reconstruction, we understood more fully how we were essentially building a new house, and the extra money we'd borrowed seemed suddenly very insubstantial. We had enough experience from previous renovation projects in the pink house to have developed a formula: triple the initial cost estimate and double the time estimate. When we finished listing the chores and calculating the costs, it was clear, if our formula held true, we'd be short on both time and money. But we'd already embarked, and we had no choice but to keep going and to trust our luck.

The House on the Top of the Hill
CUSTER COUNTY, NEBRASKA, 1958–1965

I SEE AN AUTUMN DAY, fields recently harvested, new hay stacked. My father has just pulled our new yellow Pontiac into the rutted driveway of my grandparents' farmhouse. We've driven only the length of a city block, down the hill from our house to theirs. Beside me in the backseat sit two of my younger siblings and in the front, on my mother's lap, sits the new baby. Their real names are Tamra, Cameron, and Taderic, but we call them Tami, Cam, and Tad. They don't know how to talk. Only I know how to talk. I'm three. Tami is two. Dark curls wisp about her face, and her large dark eyes scan the world from behind thick black lashes. Already I know she is much prettier than I am. Cameron is one. He is towheaded and blue-eyed, with pointy ears like one of Santa's elves. His skin is dry, and he cries a lot. My mother says he's sick with asthma. Tad, the new baby, shares my sister's dark features. They both look like our father. Tad, who is only a few weeks old, can smile at me already. I love him greedily, sometimes getting carried away and squeezing him until I shake and he cries. My mother says, "Be nice to the baby." I can't help squeezing him, though. When she isn't looking, I do it again.

This is when I first know there is a me, watching, separate, and yet a part of this place, these people. Here I am in the middle of Nebraska—the state with the funny handle sitting right in the

17

center of the country—on the eastern edge of the great Sandhills, in the dry draws and gullies of Custer County.

Long before my ancestors thought about leaving England and Germany, before any European homesteader made this a disputed territory and the site of frequent wars with the Indians, this seemingly placid terrain was the site of bloody battles between the native tribes themselves. Following the great buffalo migrations, the historic hunting grounds of several tribes overlapped in this place. They met here in fierce contests for hunting access: Kiowa, Apache, Comanche, Lakota, Cheyenne, Arapaho, Crow, Pawnee. On these plains, those tribes with the new technology of the horse eventually established dominance over the agrarian tribes. I know nothing about—nor could I possibly even imagine—this bloody past as I sit in that yellow Pontiac in 1960.

A fifth-generation Nebraskan on my father's side, I wasn't born in Nebraska. After my parents married in March of 1957, they moved to Lawton, Oklahoma, where my father was stationed during the Korean War and where I was born nine months later.

When I was six weeks old, while my parents were perhaps celebrating my first smiles on the army base in Lawton, they heard troubling reports from Nebraska. First, cryptic radio stories and, later, alarming telephone calls from their family members, all still living in the state, about a teenage killer named Charles Starkweather. My parents must have listened closely to the radio reports, trying like everyone else in the shocked nation to understand why. There appeared to be no motive, no logic, just random destruction as Starkweather's path took him west from Lincoln to just across the Wyoming border, where he was finally apprehended, leaving eleven people dead in Nebraska. My parents must have felt very far away from the danger threatening their families, both grateful for the distance and guilty for their powerlessness to help as Charlie Starkweather and his fourteen-year-old girlfriend, Caril

Ann Fugate, remained fugitives for a week at the end of January in the new year of 1958.

It would be years before I learned what Charlie Starkweather had done, but by then his name had been etched in my mind as though I'd been hearing it all my life. Although no one elaborated when they mentioned Charlie Starkweather, even as a child I associated the name with something ominous.

Maybe my ominous associations stemmed from hearing the name literally. The weather *is* stark in Nebraska. Despite its austere appearance, the plains see some of the most dramatic and randomly destructive weather systems in the world: tornadoes, hailstorms, blizzards, dust storms, thunderstorms, severe heat and severe cold, drought, and the resulting fires. The weather can change radically without warning, as it did the day of the famous blizzard in January of 1888, when a sixty-degree day turned into a raging blizzard within the space of half an hour, leaving people not only inadequately dressed but lost in the whiteout, many of them dying only feet from their own front doors. The plains environment is a legendary host to passion and disaster.

Despite this, ours was a quiet world, the wind the only pervasive sound. Always the wind. On a rare day without wind, say in summer, the air would be frenzied with birdsong: mourning doves, meadowlarks, bobwhites, cardinals, barn swallows, sparrows, red-winged blackbirds. In the house down the hill from us, where my grandparents lived, my grandmother loved the birds and often stopped in her work to listen, sometimes mimicking the bobwhite's questioning call, waiting with a faint smile for the inevitable answering whistle.

Through the screen door on such a summer day, kitchen sounds: clanging pots, slipping plates, tinkling silverware. Now, too, the rumble of a tractor as it pulls into the farmyard, the slam of a pickup door, the crow of a rooster, hens clucking and scratching in the yard around the chicken coop, a soft lowing from one of the milk cows down the hill in the corral near the house, now and then a deeper call from one of the steers in the ranch herd grazing on the surrounding pastures.

To the east and to the north we were bordered by fields—dryland crops. In the years of my childhood, milo, oats, corn, alfalfa. To the south and the west stretched acres and acres of rangeland, pasture for the large herd of beef cattle my family owned. They owned the fields full of grain, too. The rangeland was covered with buffalo grass, short and tough, green for only a few short weeks in the spring before growing gray and wiry. Scraggly red cedar trees grew in the draws, and purple-headed musk thistles were the bane of all the area ranchers. Tami, Cam, Tad, and I accompanied our grandparents on their numerous chores in the fields and the pastures. We rode along with Grandpa on the tractor, the combine, the hay loader, or in the back of the Ford pickup (a new one every two years) to check cattle: counting new calves, making certain no cows were down—a sure sign of illness or of trouble calving—checking the water tanks, and dropping off salt and mineral cubes as big as concrete blocks. We followed my grandmother into the pastures and watched her as she dug thistles or fixed fence with the post-hole digger. My father did all these chores as well, but he did them alone. He had little patience for children.

MY GRANDPARENTS met in church. My grandfather, Dale, was the new hired hand on the Charlie Samp ranch, and my grandmother, Berniece, was the second oldest daughter of Lute Samp, the minister. Charlie was her uncle. She was just a slip of girl, at seventeen barely five feet tall, with tiny feet and hands and nothing much in between. She had swarthy skin, a shy demeanor, and a brooding expression. She sang a strong, true alto in the church choir and played her violin and mandolin in the church orchestra.

Dale had come back to Nebraska after many years away. His father, always looking to get rich quick, had rented land cheap from Lakota Sioux on the Rosebud Reservation. When it became clear after several years that they'd failed in the enterprise, his father gave up, and Dale, a fourteen-year-old boy, moved his parents back to their native state. He was, by then, used to making such decisions for them.

Dale wasn't much of one for going to church, but Charlie had insisted, and so he found himself on Sunday mornings at the Nazarene church with his black hair slicked flat and his best shirt tucked into his best pants sitting in a pew holding a hymnal. He didn't join in with the singing. The singing wasn't half as bad as the sermons, though, and the sermons were nothing compared to the testimonials. If there'd ever been any possibility of conversion, it was quickly lost to the weekly testimonials. He shifted uncomfortably in his pew as local farmers and ranchers rose to confess their transgressions of the past week. In a short time, he heard confessions for sins he'd never imagined existed. And unlike everyone else who shuffled out the church door seemingly refreshed by the experience, he felt tainted by it, embarrassed by the associations he now had with certain individuals. At the door he shook Berniece's hand and ducked his head shyly as though to compensate for the difference in their height.

Berniece was shy in public, so it took him by surprise the first time he walked her home after evening services to discover how much venom she housed in that small body. She despised the church. Not only that, she harbored a deep anger toward her father. Dale thought it might have been caused by a lot of things: the hellfire and brimstone sermons; the inevitable hypocrisies; the way her father insisted she sing and play in public every Sunday, when she hated to be on display; how when she was five, her father had pushed her brusquely from his lap after her baby sister was born, saying, "You aren't the baby anymore. We have a new baby now," a betrayal she could never get past.

She had just graduated from high school. The experience had meant nothing but suffering to her. She didn't like to study, couldn't understand the merit of history or literature or math. The crowds of strange classmates had been a torment, and staying with a family not her own in the big town of Kearney was a misery she never wanted to repeat. She hadn't gotten a thing from her education, didn't see why everyone characterized it as a privilege, and now she wanted nothing so much as to leave home as fast as possible.

Dale didn't harbor this much anger, but he took Berniece's anger seriously. He was impressed with her anger as much as he was impressed with her talents. He was a little embarrassed by her education; he had completed only the eighth grade himself. That couldn't be helped. He tried to explain how his father, never well, had needed him to start contributing to the family income from a young age. Many mornings his mother greeted him with the news that his father wouldn't be going out to help with morning chores, explaining, "Dickie isn't feeling well today." Berniece, no longer shy with him, made her opinion clear. His father was a wastrel and a fake, she told him. He'd been using him all his life. Dale had never considered this possibility. He was taken aback by both her vehemence and this new way of seeing his own life. Her anger was infectious. Within a short period of time, it became clear to them that they were surrounded by people whose intentions toward them were less than good.

Dale could work all day like one of the animals on the farm, but Berniece didn't know until after they were married that he stayed up till all hours reading books: military or western romances. He couldn't bear to stop in the middle of an adventure. What she did know was that he was a not bad-looking man, if a little daft about some things. He had a certain flair she admired, buckling his belt on the side, some fad from the reservation. He didn't have a plan, only a strong back and a sweet disposition. She had a plan, and she guessed he was just the man to help her realize it.

They were married in September of 1932, after which they took a short honeymoon—two days and a night—to Loup City, forty miles east, where they visited the Jenner's Zoological, Educational, and Amusement Park. The autumn days were golden, still warm. They'd never seen so many people in one place, more than three thousand of them. They saw exotic animals—plumed birds, peacocks, monkeys, snakes from the tropics—and were amazed by collections of every kind imaginable: guns, rare musical instruments, inlaid chests, rare books, and Egyptian mummies. In the park, lush with trees, flowers, walks, and lawns, were bowling galleries, shooting galleries, and a strange undulating ride called the "Ocean Wave." The buildings that housed the collections were themselves a sight to behold: pagodas, Thai temples, an Alaskan Indian hut, an Egyptian-style pavilion; and scattered on the grounds were totem poles, figures carved in stone and wood, a fat, contemplative Buddha.

Their first act as a married couple was to leave the church— Berniece proclaiming as she left that if she ever had a son and he became a minister, she'd disown him. The second thing they did was start saving for a place of their own. The two years they waited, they stayed with Dale's parents, running their farm for them. Just as Berniece had suspected from the beginning, both of Dale's parents were all too willing to let others work on their behalf. Berniece had a new resentment she set smoldering; as long as her in-laws lived, they'd be an unnecessary and unfair burden. Dale, she soon enough discovered, lacked the strength to stand up to them. There was something soft in him toward others, and something stubborn, too. This was one matter on which he refused to budge.

Nine months after their wedding, their only child, a son they named Gerald, was born on the kitchen table at Dale's parent's house. Dale, who had assisted the doctor from town, never recovered from the sight of Berniece "all trussed up like a turkey," bellowing and cursing him for her troubles even as the baby moved out from between her bloody thighs.

She blamed him later for the pain, could never seem to forgive him for it; and a combination of his own repulsive memories of that night and the ways she seemed to warn him away affected their intimacy for a long, long time. The boy, my father, became an excuse. He slept in their room, first in a crib, later on a cot, until at age fourteen he asked for his own room.

In the first years of their marriage, Berniece's entire family sold their land, their animals, their tools, and their machines and moved away to various points west: Colorado, Idaho, Oregon. Before leaving, they urged Berniece and Dale to join them in their exodus. They didn't stop urging even as they stood at farm auctions and watched their history sold piece by piece. The wind blew, and the dust choked them, as they dreamed about their escape from this godforsaken country.

Dale didn't say much in response to them. It was Berniece who always made it clear they weren't following anyone anywhere. Instead, they quietly bought up those acres of land everyone else thought were worthless, Dale working in Iowa during the corn harvest to earn extra money for those purchases. The years of drought and blowing dust left few survivors. "Anyone who stays must be stubborn or crazy or both" was the last word from the Samp family as they exited the state.

Things only got worse in the dry years. And if from time to time Dale questioned the rightness of their decision, he still pushed on, buying finally a farmhouse a half section away from his parents, who had by then grown accustomed to being cared for by the young couple, insisting on such care for the rest of their lives.

Although Roosevelt's New Deal was the only way they all kept from starving, it was a confusion to them and a blow to their pride to have to buy from the government their own hogs fattened on their own place and to do the same with the milk their cows produced and the eggs their chickens laid. They were determined they'd never need to rely on anyone again.

Many years later, my grandparents bought my parents a house at the top of the hill, within view of their own house. They painted both houses the same. In addition to caring for the four of us, my mother took care of the chickens and the house. I see her still, carrying galvanized buckets of feed and water to the chicken coop across the drive on the east side of our farmyard. I see her in winter wearing a green plaid wool coat. I see her from my second-story bedroom window while I'm supposed to be napping, home from kindergarten, where I'm the youngest child on the school bus each day. For a while I make a terrible scene each afternoon, throwing open the bedroom window and screaming in terror when I see her at her daily chores. I'm unable, for a few weeks, to understand she's walking to the chicken coop and not toward the road, that it's a bucket she carries and not a suitcase. I'm convinced she's leaving us. Although she can't at first understand me, she eventually makes out my screams, "Don't make me an orphan!"

The concept of orphans is new to me, freshly gleaned knowledge from a cover of *The Weekly Reader* featuring sad-faced children looking up woefully, hungrily at the camera. The title: "Orphans." My simple question: "What's an orphan?" My mother's innocent reply: "Children whose parents have left them." And a startling new realization such a horror is possible. It was the beginning, the shock of education. Before then I couldn't have imagined a world in which parents might leave. Now I knew they could and feared wildly, absolutely, the stunning possibility of abandonment. The worst thing that could happen.

THE LAND IN NEBRASKA may be as some describe it—flat, boring, austere—but it was not the land that interested me so much as the dramatic and dynamic presence of the sky. The sky was much more vast than the land, the astonishing and mutable clouds like continents or ships drifting above us. We were erased in that great expanse, and beneath it we knew our place. We were all but annihilated under the burden of the sky. Nothing broke the view. Nothing stopped the sky from horizon to horizon. No direction was distinct from another. We were always aware of our place there, our minuscule lives. We didn't talk about ideas. The grand questions of life seemed trivial and absurd beneath that endless, obliterating sky. Who would have listened if we'd spoken? Our voices didn't return to us but went on and on.

And the wind, the *basso ostinato* of our lives, the ever-present wind. As the seasons cycled in thematic sequence, it was always against the background of the wind, the variations of their themes marked by the wind's constant pulse. In summer the curtains in our house billowed and flew, the screens were plucked and released, the edges of the doors whistled. In winter, the wind stalked about the house knocking against the wooden frame like a giant hitting it with his shoulder. The dust was everywhere. We all but disappeared.

The house on the top of the hill was so isolated that many days the only passing car was that driven by the mailman. On nice days, my siblings and I, giddy about seeing him, watched from the yard and scrambled madly to the front porch, where we could wave at him as he stopped on the road. We watched as he put the mail in the box at the end of the driveway, delighted when he waved back to us as he pulled away. It was more than just human company we craved; it was the gifts he left. With the mail he often left us a pack of Blackjack or Clove gum. None of us liked the strong taste of the licorice- or clove-flavored gums (the only kind he ever brought), but we chewed the entire packet and fought over the single remaining stick every time. We couldn't refuse this gift from outside. Strangers were rare, and we cherished what they brought even if it was distasteful. The unknown, I had discovered, was always better than the familiar. Even then, I understood it was a curse to be limited to one life. I craved an experience of other lives, other times, other places. I must have known already that I would be a reader, a writer, hungry to learn, that I would eventually relinquish the familiar for the exotic gifts of strangers.

OUR OLD FARMHOUSE had many rooms and plenty of space and time for solitude. In addition to the bedrooms upstairs was a secret room that could be reached only through a hallway inside a bedroom closet. My father was a hunter, and this room was where he made fancy gunstocks and loaded his own shotgun shells at night. I wasn't allowed in that room, its shadowy contours glimpsed only occasionally and always furtively. At night I sometimes woke to see my father coming or going from that room—for it was the closet of the bedroom I shared with my sister that housed the hallway leading to the secret room. Once, the large black wood-burning stove that warmed our bedroom became a bear. In the darkness I woke hearing my father and saw a bear instead.

Downstairs were airy rooms, a large kitchen where we ate, a walk-in pantry, my parents' bedroom, a long living room, and a sunny den with windows and French doors facing the orchard my father had planted.

Behind our house stood a teetering red barn that leaned visibly to the west. One afternoon men from area farms and ranches came and, working together, pushed the red barn over. It sank and settled upon itself with a slow moaning grace, the dust rising before slowly filtering back to the ground. Long before its dramatic demise, no animals had been kept in the barn. Instead, my father had built a modern one-story barn to the west, halfway down the hill and not visible from the house.

The barn on my grandparents' place down the hill, because it was old, housed smells acquired through the years: manure and hay, feed and calf formula. On the sill of the dusty window sat a green can of Bag Balm. When it was opened, its sharp minty smell momentarily erased all other smells in the barn. Outside the open door, swallows dove from their nests under the barn's eaves, their yellow bellies flashing in the sun. The haymow was a twilit place. Worn wooden boards had been nailed crosswise to the barn wall where they served as a ladder. When I climbed to that darkness, the musk of old hay and wood made me want to sleep. Before I was born, my grandparents had a pet coyote named Bill, who, Grandpa claimed, would not only help herd pigs but would climb that ladder to sleep in the haymow.

The adults around me talked about the weather—rain, snow, hail, sleet, drought, thaws, freezes. They worried about plant diseases and animal diseases. They discussed the maintenance of machines: combines, planters, manure spreaders, discs, milk machines, cream separators, grain trucks, cattle trucks, hay loaders, tractors, threshers. I didn't know what most of these machines did, but they were among the first words in my lexicon.

While living in the house at the top of the hill, I began to see there were two worlds, what was inside my head and what was outside. The things inside were secret things—night dreams and thoughts, ideas, and daydreams with imaginary people and places; outside was everything else. No one talked about the inside things. I liked the things inside my head best. Before I could read or write, my drawings were stories. When I thought no one was around, I played wild uninhibited songs on the piano, a massive converted player piano, dark with old varnish. These songs were stories too. I wanted to be every character in every story. I didn't want to be just me.

My one passionate interaction, outside of my own imaginative play and that with my siblings, was with animals. Among them were our milk cows, a motley lot acquired in an apparently haphazard way, only a few of which I remember: a blue roan, a leggy jersey, a red cow with horns named Daisy, and a tall, bony Holstein. On windless days I liked to sit on the fence of the corral and watch these cows. I sometimes sang to them.

I found out how cows become food by accident at my grandparents' house. I was sitting alone on a haystack near the barn when a gunshot rang out. I looked up in time to see my grandfather still pointing a revolver at a black steer. In the same instant that I glanced up, my father jumped from where he'd been sitting on the fence and cut the steer's throat in one quick, almost beautiful, fluid motion. The steer's knees buckled, and it let out a bawling gasp as blood gushed from its neck and poured across its huge chest. Later, my father was furious with my hysterics. I wasn't a child to recover easily from such a shock.

Not long before this, at age seven, I'd been given a black Angus calf and told it would be my 4-H project. I loved that calf, his thick pink tongue, his soft lips, his long eyelashes and beautiful, dark eyes, his coal black coat. He was very young, an orphaned calf, I now see, since he had to be bottle-fed. I fed him with my father's help and hovered over him where he lay on the straw in the barn, a light provided for warmth. It was spring and still chilly.

Had I been allowed to raise this calf, I might have learned, as so many other ranch kids do, the harsh realities of the world of food production, for the calf the child nurtures by hand, grooms and fattens, trains to the halter, names and loves as a pet is doomed to be sold at the close of the county fair to the meat producer. I wonder if in fact I would have learned from this experience, as other ranch children seem to, that the world is not as we imagine it. I wonder if it would have prepared me to take my place in the ranch economy. I'll never know.

In the house at the top of the hill, things were changing. My father was changing. He was moving away from his childhood in the house at the bottom of the hill, and we would all be different because of it. In the fall of my seventh year, my Angus calf was only a few months old when my family left the house on the top of the hill to move to Litchfield, the small town nearby where I went to school. It would become the first leg of my father's fruitless odyssey to find happiness.

Before we moved, I was told I could take along only one of the thirteen farm kittens I'd tamed that summer. After that, I played with my kittens under the grim prospect of that choice. Suddenly they had to be singled out and scrutinized. I chose a dark tabby kitten I'd named Star because of the irregular yellow patch on his forehead. Star wasn't my favorite. He was, in fact, far from my favorite. My favorite was obviously Snowball, a pure white long-haired, breathtakingly perfect kitten. Or maybe it was Puff (because of the books I'd read in school that year), a black and white shorthair whose outgoing personality meant he was always on my lap. Star, meanwhile, had stayed on the fringes, only one of thirteen, not singled out before. No matter why I'd chosen him, Star it was, and, given my mother's dislike for cats, I knew I was lucky to be taking any kitten.

Star wouldn't live out the winter at the new house. Within weeks of our move, he died of distemper. I imagined then the other twelve kittens were still safe there in the country alone. I imagined them free and happy. I consoled myself that way, thankful to have spared Snowball or Puff what surely would have awaited one of them had I chosen what I most wanted instead.

My grandparents stayed on the ranch for another decade after we left, and over the years while visiting them, I returned again and again to the house we still owned on the top of the hill, where it sat empty. I trudged alone or with one or more of my younger siblings. The corrals grew thick with weeds, and the buildings weathered to gray. Badgers built their dens beneath the front porch. I never knew what I was looking for on those visits, some part of myself perhaps, some way I'd betrayed the part of myself I'd left there, the ways I'd turned my back on what I loved most.

October 2001

OCTOBER IN NEBRASKA can be raw, windy, and miserable. Fortunately, October of 2001 wasn't. Instead, the wind was still, the sky a vivid, cloudless blue, the earth suffused with sunlight. Life went on as usual, and it was much too early for us to fully understand how our lives would change in the year to come. The work ahead was still theoretical, and the sheer exhaustion of it an abstraction. We discussed the problem of time, for we felt our lives were already busy and we couldn't imagine how a project of this magnitude would fit into our already full schedules.

Noel's work was seasonally hectic. As the operations manager of a grain elevator, he was responsible for both storing and shipping grain. October is the beginning of harvest in Nebraska, and he and his crew were ramping up for at least six weeks of overtime hours—seven days a week, twelve-, sometimes fifteen-hour days. Through the winter, there would be trains to load, often in the dead of night. In order to meet strict railroad deadlines they loaded no matter the hour or the severity of the weather, and they didn't know even vaguely when the trains would arrive, so he was often on call. Maybe the biggest question before us now was how Noel would find time for work on the house while still meeting the demands of his job.

The grain elevator where Noel worked was a small branch operation of a large grain corporation, and his crew totaled five. Tall, lean Noel and four burly men: Rick (sometimes called Taco for his Mexican surname), Tracy (a shy, competent man, who had worked at the elevator since he was a teenager), Rodney (an African American man, who had moved his family to Nebraska from Mississippi), and Mike (the youngest member of the crew, given to rescuing small animals and fond of singing karaoke). Noel referred to them as "the ladies." Although he intended to be ironic, in a sense they were "the ladies," a description that would have had to include Noel as well. It wasn't only their tendency to talk to one another about everything—health and family problems, home repairs, all purchases major and minor—or their fastidious complaints to one another. It was also their habit of watching together the daytime soap opera "The Young and the Restless" during their lunch hour, a habit they apparently shared with some of the truckers who hauled corn and soybeans in and out of their facility. Now and then Rick could be overheard on the radio having a spirited conversation with a trucker about one of the show's characters or numerous plot lines.

A friend of ours had recently written a piece about the guys at the grain elevator, which had aired on NPR's *This American Life*. Writer friends across the country heard it, and although Noel was never identified in the essay, they knew immediately it had to be his elevator being profiled.

In the summer the guys sometimes planned potlucks together, grilling hamburgers or steaks, each contributing side dishes from home. The nature of their work was physically demanding, often dangerous. They loaded and unloaded trucks, moved grain from bin to bin, and loaded trains, but mostly they cleaned. Their most relentless job was sweeping, and annually they went through dozens of brooms. A dirty grain elevator is a dangerous grain elevator, and dust must be kept to a minimum. Grain dust is a volatile element, as explosive as gunpowder, and something as innocuous as the random spark from a backfiring truck can set off a series of explosions as grain dust combusts, causing elevators to blow up.

Noel wasn't born into this life. It's something he'd chosen after first working two summers on his cousin's farm, returning in the winters to his home in San Francisco. Eventually, he gave up his San Francisco apartment and left the city he loved to settle in Nebraska. Farm work led naturally to work in the grain elevator. He was sometimes surprised himself at how long he'd remained interested in agriculture, but he admitted he'd grown tired of the city and Nebraska fulfilled the longing he had for a simpler life. Noel's father, Floyd, had been relieved at eighteen to escape his boyhood in Nebraska, and not surprisingly Noel had grown up seeing Nebraska as an unlikely place to move. But inexplicably here he was, back again among his father's people, the farmers of Nebraska, and loving them, their sly irony, their dry sense of humor, their stubbornness, and their impatience with pretensions of any kind.

THE FIRST PURCHASE for the job ahead, we decided, had to be a truck. Noel had sold his 1969 Ford pickup the year before, and although he drove a company truck, he knew it wouldn't be appropriate for hauling building materials and debris back and forth through the winter. Since the end of September, he'd been looking for and now finally found the right vehicle: a 1982 Chevy four-wheel drive. It was a mess to look at—rust, coated with unpainted gray primer. Still, the price was fair, and most importantly, Noel trusted it to be a reliable vehicle. I balked a bit as we wrote out the check for that purchase. Already I knew in the months to come I'd be struggling with anxiety about all the huge purchases we'd be making. We're not financial risk takers. We tend to buy used rather than new, thinking long and hard before making big purchases.

Waiting to become owners of the country house and to begin the work ahead of us was hard for Noel, and as the month went on, he grew restless. It was tempting at times to second-guess ourselves. When our friend from Pittsburgh came to visit, he went with Noel to the country house to post No Hunting signs around the property. Ingrid had happily obliged Noel's request to post the signs although we weren't yet the official owners of the house.

This outing was Noel's first chance to walk through the entire property, and he couldn't have had a better companion for doing it. Our friend loved the place and eagerly explored with Noel, even examining the contents of the dump they found on the southwest edge of the property, where ancient farm implements rusted among household appliances, an old VW, several bicycle frames, and all kinds of items disposed of over the years.

Noel had felt sick when he'd first seen the dumpsite. Not understanding it was common among rural households in the past century to dispose of refuse in this way, he thought he'd have to deal with it immediately. "No," our friend had said. "You don't have to get rid of this unless you want to. You can't see it from the house, and it isn't hurting anything."

That day served as a turning point for Noel in regard to the property, and instead of being consumed with questions, he was instead reassured our decision had been a wise one and felt eager to get started. He told me that evening about what he'd seen on his earlier walk. "The place is perfect," he added. I was glad for his contentment, but I didn't yet feel in sync with his assessment. He was so happy, though, so excited about the life he saw us living there, I wanted to believe him. I certainly didn't want to share my own doubts.

In mid-October Noel met the bank's inspector at the country house. Ingrid guardedly let them in to look around. Noel had accompanied him both to get a more thorough look at the place inside and to reassure the inspector about what we were planning. As they made their way through the house, even though the inspector understood what we meant to do, he was so overwhelmed by the house's numerous problems he finally stopped remarking on them. Noel, however, was relieved things weren't any worse than he'd initially suspected.

Despite understanding our plans, the inspector felt obligated to write a rudimentary report. Later, Noel told me, as the inspector read his report, Ingrid was visibly uncomfortable. This had been her home after all. "I felt bad for her," Noel said, but then his face brightened as he went on to recall how while they'd all been standing together in front of the house, the inspector had stopped talking to watch in amazement with Noel and Ingrid as a deer and her fawn walked casually across the lawn not ten feet from them. Afterward, Ingrid had shrugged. "They always come into the yard. They aren't afraid at all."

On two other occasions in the month of October, Noel and I returned together to the country house at Ingrid's request. She wanted to give us some things: files on the work she'd had done in the house, information about the house's quirks, a list of the birds she'd documented seeing through the years, and finally, we came to understand, she wanted to give us the stories of her life on this place, which she called Serenity Acres. She talked about her ex-husband and about her three boys, all now estranged from her. She talked about the problems she'd had with local vendors and the dreams she'd had for improving the house and the property. She showed us where her vegetable garden used to be—now completely overgrown and indistinguishable from the other weedy areas around it—and where her herb garden had once been, also overgrown beyond recognition. She walked us up beyond the granary into the meadow, where she pointed out the remains of a sweat lodge her ex-husband and his Lakota Sioux friends had built.

When it started collapsing a few years earlier, Ingrid asked her ex-husband to come dismantle it. "There's a ritual for taking it down," she explained to us. "I didn't want to do it without that ritual." But her ex-husband had never returned, and all that remained of the sweat lodge now was a fire pit, a brush pile, and an old tarp. Sweet grass grew in this meadow, she said, and it was sacred to the Lakota. In front of the house, two flat cedar trees stood like guardians at the door. They were sacred, too. I knew without exchanging a glance with Noel those two scraggly trees would go. I felt a little guilty for the thought, but only for a moment. Respecting another's sacred tradition is not the same as adopting it.

Later that day as we sat together at the picnic table in the warm autumn sun, listening while Ingrid went through each page in her house file, she suddenly said, "I think I've killed all the rats in the crawl space under the living room." We didn't respond to this comment, and she went on. "When they poured the new basement, they left a hole in the concrete, and rats got into the crawl space." She didn't seem to notice what I know must have been a look of alarm on my face. Noel refused to look at me and instead calmly nodded as Ingrid admitted she'd finally had to use poison. "I tried to patch the concrete," she gestured toward the foundation, "but they just dug through."

Still calm, Noel said, "You'd have to add glass to the concrete to keep them from getting through," and I supposed he was mentally adding that repair to his list of things to do. Among my concerns about the move was my morbid fear of mice. Rats were off the scale. In my mind, country living equaled rodents, and Noel had spent not a few conversations in the past month since we'd bought the place assuring me he'd make the country house as tight as he possibly could against mice. I knew even as Ingrid was speaking that the rats had not been confined to the crawl space. Suddenly the substantial hole in the baseboard of the living room, noticeable despite the bricks she'd laid against it, was all the evidence I needed to know those rats had been *inside* the house—and a steady supply of birdseed all the enticement they needed to stay.

A couple of weeks later on the evening of the 29th, I was thinking about those rats while we were driving to the house for the first time as its official owners, having signed the closing papers earlier that day. When we pulled into the drive, I forgot all about the rats as we saw Ingrid had not yet moved out. She was there with a friend, beside herself, fussing over details. She stopped vacuuming when we walked in, and she continued to worry aloud about the need to leave the house clean for us. "When I moved the buffet in the dining room," she told us distractedly, "there was so much dust." Neither Noel nor I had the heart to tell her the dust she was fretting over would pale by comparison to the mess the house was about to become. We failed to convince her she didn't need to clean anymore and finally decided to leave. Her friend gave us an understanding smile and quietly assured us Ingrid would be out by the next morning.

We were disappointed as we left that evening. We hadn't had a chance to do the careful inventory of the country house as we'd hoped. Maybe to console ourselves, we took the long way home, driving gravel roads back to Lincoln.

While the east/west roads around the country house had interesting names—the Princeton Road to the north and the Pella Road to the south, beyond those roads the Olive Creek Road, Panama Road, Gage Road, and Firth Road—no matter how many times I said our new address to myself, South 25th Street was a disappointment. The five-digit house number seemed absurd even with the knowledge that it had been formulated for emergency rescue units. Then, too, the new postal address was Martell, a town several miles away and the least charming of the small towns in the area.

The country house was nearest the unincorporated town of

Princeton with its smattering of houses, its serene old country grain elevator, a landmark for miles, its well-maintained small cemetery, and its tavern. The Princeton tavern was a place where neighborhood families gathered, the life of the surrounding area. The space was filled with scattered dining tables and a couple of pool tables. Booths lined the east wall while against the west wall the bar sat at an odd angle like a broken wing against the west wall. An impressive beer can collection lined the south and east walls. Once we'd discovered the tavern's excellent food, our hearts sank to see the For Sale sign in the window shortly after we bought the house. We couldn't imagine who would assume such a responsibility and feared it would go the way of so many other businesses in rural areas and stand empty.

The following morning Ingrid was gone as promised, and Noel returned alone that evening after work to start removing the tops of the two chimneys. The next day, the roofing crew was on site as planned. They finished the roof in two days while Noel continued to remove the remainder of the chimneys, carefully stacking the bricks in the backyard for the day when they might be useful to build a patio or walks, all dreams for the far distant future. I felt sometimes it took equal parts imagination and nutty faith to believe in that finished house with its L-shaped front porch, its garden and patio out back. But most of the time I did believe in it, even if my belief seemed suspended at the point of actually seeing myself happy in it.

When we drove the kids out to look at the house for the first time a few days later, they'd had time to adjust to the idea. They didn't say much as we pulled into the drive, nor later as they walked quietly through the house. They were so reticent I finally asked what they were thinking. Jordan shrugged, "You two will make it nice." Leif smiled. "It'll be a good place to come for Christmas." Finnegan had come along with us, and the kids quickly tired of being inside and went out to romp with him. I watched them running through the tall grass and weeds, Finnegan bounding ahead as though showing them around. Jordan and Bronwyn are both strawberry blondes, and Leif is a true redhead. Blue-eyed and with a spattering of freckles across their noses, they're unmistakably siblings. Already the country place seemed a little bit more like home to me with them there laughing together.

House on the Gravel Road
LITCHFIELD, NEBRASKA, 1965–1967

AT THE AGE OF NINE, I had my first epiphany. It was in my fourth-grade classroom. I remember the pale blue, dotted-swiss dress I was wearing as I played with my best friend Rhonda. Rhonda had just told me she thought she looked like a donkey, and I saw that indeed she did have very large ears, though I knew she was beautiful. Rhonda didn't tell me this as a way of feeling sorry for herself. She preferred animals to people, and she'd been pretending to be a donkey as we played that day. The sun streamed through the windows of the garden-level classroom as I glanced up to see through the glass the feet of the high school students passing on the sidewalk outside. Somehow this combination of events stopped time in a way that would eventually become familiar to me but which then seemed new and startling. I saw in that split second how I, too, would someday be one of those older students passing by unaware of being observed, how I, too, would grow up and move on, how I would not always play the games I was playing now.

When my family left the house on the top of the hill, it was to move to a house on a gravel road on the outskirts of Litchfield (pop. 253). Across from us was the school's football field and beside the house an empty lot full of ragweed, dock, nettles, milkweed, tall prairie grasses, and volunteer mulberry and elm. I imagined it was a forest. My sister Tami and I built secret paths and playhouses in those weeds, far away from the world of adults. The house itself,

41

a simple bungalow, sat on a wide wooded lot. Beside the detached garage grew tiger lilies and hollyhocks, and in the backyard stood an ancient oak tree. From behind its thick trunk, my siblings and I liked to spy on our neighbors, the Slocums. From the beginning, we tormented them. We rang their doorbell and ran. We sang loudly from a branch of the oak tree that reached into their yard. When they were very young, my brothers once picked every flower in the Slocums' flower garden.

If as kids we were badly behaved, it seemed Dad was little better. Still thinking he was on the ranch, he decided to raise two wild turkeys that first year and, considering them pets rather than livestock, didn't confine them as he should have until after they got into the Slocums' garden and destroyed all their tomato plants.

The house on the gravel road was only two blocks from the gas station Dad had bought on Highway 2, newly christened Randy's 66. We were more involved in his life at this time as we came and went in the gas station—pulling bottles of chocolate or strawberry Nehi soda from the ice cold water of the old-fashioned pop dispenser or eating Almond Joy or Bit 'O Honey or Snickers bars after school.

Whenever I think about the gas station, I picture a winter afternoon, a slow day (maybe they were all slow days). The concrete floor of the station has been newly painted with slick gray porch paint. I'm sitting beside the wood-burning stove Dad has installed to warm the uninsulated building. Outside, the wind bangs the metal signs advertising motor oil and fan belts. Dad sits in his heavy office chair, his feet up on the desk. We're watching Harry— the black rabbit he's acquired as the gas station pet. Every morning Dad cleans up the night's accumulation of rabbit droppings and checks the telephone cords. Harry likes to chew through the wires. Outside, against the stark blue Nebraska winter sky, I see the pink granite wishing well and birdbath some optimistic previous owner built to attract potential customers.

When Mom opened the Swirl-a-Cone—a summer ice-cream drive-in attached to the back of the gas station—my siblings and I spent summer days playing on the grassy tree-shaded lot behind the gas station. The drive-in was a big success. Mom sold hamburgers, hotdogs, French fries, deep-fried chicken, shrimp-in-a-basket, and soft ice cream: sundaes, cones, malts, and a few strange, lavish concoctions of her own, including the Pig's Party (a banana split without the banana) and the Deluxe Sundae (ice cream topped with butterscotch and covered with a hard chocolate shell). A small sliding window served customers outside, and a counter with a small seating area served customers inside. I was allowed to work in the drive-in when I turned nine. I loved the feeling of taking orders and competently filling them, making a perfect swirl of ice cream on the end of a cone, lowering metal mesh baskets of frozen French fries, breaded shrimp, or chicken into hot grease, the oil sputtering and popping with the shock of the cold, and knowing just by watching when they were done.

In the small dining area, my parents' friend, the local high school art teacher, had painted a mural featuring an exotic scene: pink flamingos against a background of tropical greenery and a turquoise sea. I now think of the adults living in that small town as far from the tropics and the sea as they could be and how that mural seemed to capture all their longings.

Mom's way with people and her efficiency in any endeavor made the restaurant a hit, but it didn't keep the gas station from failing. In fact, the gas station was already a losing proposition when Dad bought it, for that same year the new Interstate 80 steadily funneled east-west traffic away from formerly busy Highway 2.

THE ICE-CREAM DRIVE-IN didn't make deliveries, but one autumn night late in the season, shortly before it closed for the winter, Mom sent me and my brother Cam to deliver a small dish of plain soft-serve vanilla to a tiny house at the end of the block. An enormous blue spruce filled the entire front yard, and its bottom branches, like a long full skirt, seemed intent on sweeping the little house beneath them. The night was dark. A hazy, half moon glowed in the humid night sky, and the air was balmy, thick with the acrid smell of burning leaves.

We were timid as we approached the house. We'd never seen the old woman who lived there, and the house looked empty as we went to the back door where we'd been instructed to go. Fallen leaves rustled against the foundation. "She's a witch," Cam whispered to me as we waited, and I felt my heart clutch with fear, for I, too, had heard the stories; but I was the older sister, and I couldn't give in to my fear. I shushed him.

When the old woman finally answered our knock, I was almost overcome by the stuffy close heat and a strong sickly sweet smell I couldn't identify. She beckoned to us silently, and we followed her through a tunnel of newspapers stacked high along the walls on either side of the back porch. Barefoot, she wore a white nightgown that fell to the floor. Her long, gauzy white hair hung down below her hips. She didn't speak, and in the silence we heard a strange clacking on the linoleum floor as she walked ahead of us. When our gaze followed the sound, we saw her toenails had grown long and thick, yellow and curved like a dog's claws.

She gestured for us to set the ice cream on the table; it had started to melt in its blue plastic dish. I noticed she'd been eating breakfast cereal for supper, and half a bowl sat unfinished on the table. Her blue eyes were runny and unfocused as she looked up at us. She held a small, black leather, clasp purse close against her body and with trembling fingers pulled out several coins. The coins smelled strongly of the same odd odor in the house, and later when I handed them to Mom, the smell stayed on my hands.

That fall, I went door to door selling Christmas cards. I met my sales goal and earned a gold Sting-Ray, the first Sting-Ray bike in the town of Litchfield. It sported three speeds, a wheelie bar, and a shiny metallic gold banana seat. That year I also acquired a used alto saxophone and played in the town's tiny grade-school band. Its reddish-gold tone and white mouthpiece set it apart from newer saxophones. I'd been taking piano lessons since I was five and could sight-read well. Perhaps because of this skill, I felt I didn't need to practice, and each week Mom was embarrassed to sign a practice sheet filled with zeros.

The three summers we lived in the house on the gravel road we attended Vacation Bible School at the Christian Church, where all day for a week we made crafts and sang songs and listened to Bible stories. After lunch each day we played on the grassy lawn beside the church. To this day, whenever I read the balcony scene of *Romeo and Juliet*, I invariably conjure that churchyard. I think it must have something to do with Jimmy Goodner. He attended a country school and didn't go to our church, so during the year the only time I saw handsome Jimmy Goodner was the week of Vacation Bible School. My affectionate memories of VBS must surely be tied to the tingly feeling I felt in his presence. Every activity was colored by that emotion. The feeling, it seemed, was reciprocal, and through the course of the week we grew bolder until the last day, when on a sort of dare we met and kissed on the green church lawn during the recess after lunch.

My friend Tim attended church each Sunday with Ed and Della Banker. They didn't really adopt him, but he lived with them most of the time. His was the only Native American family in town. They lived near the Bankers in a small, unpainted house. Chained to a heavy stake, a half-mad German shepherd paced their yard bare.

In first grade, Tim was hurt one day during recess. His leg got caught in the center of the moving merry-go-round. We, his classmates, had all seen the way his leg was twisted in the accident and believed him when he told the teacher he thought he'd broken it. The teacher disagreed. She mocked him when she noticed him limping, somehow suggesting he was faking. I'd never seen anything in Tim's prior behavior to indicate he would fake an injury, nor had I seen an adult treat a child in this way. The next morning when Tim arrived at school on crutches, his leg completely encased in a cast, the class ran to admire it. The teacher, as I recall, said nothing.

I'd been slow to see it, but I eventually realized school was about competition. Reading groups were assigned by color. Math flash cards ferreted out the slackers as we stood in teams of two confronting the multiplication question the teacher held in front of us. In gym, dodge ball left only the quick and the ruthless standing alone. In band we were assigned seats according to our skill.

We were all very aware of our class standing. Those who were different were singled out mercilessly. Although I'd always hated to see kids teased on the playground, the ranking system in the classroom—because they were decisions made by adults—had always seemed acceptable. Students appeared to deserve their place in the established pecking order of the classroom. I trusted the teachers to know these things. The nose pickers, the paste and paper eaters, the slow, the confused seemed justifiably last in every category, while the beautiful, the talented, and the quick seemed in their rightful place at the top. After the episode with Tim, though, I felt my former confidence slip as I realized teachers, too, played games, as cruel as those played by children.

One of the games I was playing at that time was a great fabrication. Over the course of a few months, the game had taken on a life of its own and had evolved into a kind of cosmology for a small group of girls in my class. Always the storyteller among my friends, my obsession with this particular cycle of stories had begun with drawings I'd made of girls and the detailed biographies I'd devised for them. These girls, I convinced myself, lived among the stars, and I could communicate with them. With these stories, I eventually persuaded a group of my friends that they, too, could communicate with the Star Girls. I created an elaborate tale about how we could transmit messages through the birthstone bracelets popular that year, bracelets conveniently owned by all of us.

When I first described the Star Girls and showed my friends the drawings I'd made and the stories I'd written, they accepted them without question. I'd anticipated teasing, but not one of them challenged or questioned me. Nor did they resist when months later I announced our Star Girls were going to help us fly. Instead, my friends ran full on and jumped with me over a steep embankment behind our school playground. We solemnly flapped our arms that day even as our feet hit the ground hard and all of us ran headlong to the bottom barely keeping ourselves upright. Afterward, we were disappointed, but together we compiled several possible explanations as to why we hadn't been able to fly, none of which included criticism of me or my harebrained ideas. No one hinted at the pos- . sibility the Star Girls didn't exist. It appeared that no one, especially me, wanted to give up believing in girls from outer space.

I wasn't the first inhabitant of Nebraska to look to the stars for answers. The Skiri Pawnee tribe, who had inhabited central Nebraska since as far back as the eighteenth century, developed a complex religion based on the cosmos. The Pawnee star religion demanded from time to time a human sacrifice—the only North American native tribe to perform human sacrifices. The Morning Star ritual, as it was called, started with a dream and before being implemented had to be confirmed by complex signs in the stars. They always sacrificed a young girl, a captive from another tribe. Before the sacrifice she was treated as an honored guest, living with the tribe for weeks, even months, until the heavens indicated the time was right.

The most populous of the Native American tribes in Nebraska, the Pawnee had domesticated the horse early in the eighteenth century and were accomplished hunters as well as expert farmers. In the nineteenth century, shortly before the first European settlers came to the area in large numbers, the Pawnee sold millions of acres of their historical tribal lands to the federal government for almost nothing; but they'd perhaps had little choice, the tribe having been decimated by a hundred years of smallpox outbreaks, hunger, and forced relocations.

By the time my maternal great-grandparents settled in Nebraska on what had been Pawnee land, the Pawnee were mostly gone, and in their place Polish immigrants had put down roots. In pictures, my great-grandmother, Ida Hope Stickney, is clearly the matriarch—her thick white hair worn like a crown. She was considered something of a witch by those living in what had by then been dubbed the Dead Horse Canyon (named for an infantry caught in the valley during a blizzard while en route between forts). I've been told that men from the area came to her for advice about everything from planting to investing. Meanwhile, my great-grandfather, a wiry little boxer, had quickly learned that winning boxing matches against his Polish neighbors wasn't a good long-term strategy for success. He built a two-story barn and hired Polish bands to play for dances there every Saturday night. He was also known for making and sharing his homemade hooch.

I never knew my maternal grandmother, Alice, except through my mother's stories. One of twelve children (seven girls and five boys), she was singled out because of a weak heart, diagnosed when she was a child. Spared the heavy farm chores and many of the household tasks, she was sent to school instead and alone among her siblings finished high school.

My grandmother had wandered as a child in the Dead Horse

Canyon, finding arrowheads and old buttons from cavalry uni-
forms. Growing up, she must have heard stories about the Pawnee. It's likely she knew about the Pawnee star religion, how they
believed that when their people died, they ascended to the heavens
where, in the form of stars, they watched over the tribe. Every decision the tribe made—planting, harvesting, hunting—was based
on the position of the stars (the advice of their ancestors). How
could she not have heard about the Morning Star ritual? How the
sacrifice was always a thirteen-year-old girl they'd captured from
another tribe. How any man in the tribe who dreamt of the Morning Star and woke to see the star the next morning was required
to make the sacrifice. How the man who'd had such a dream and
its confirmation, it is said, woke the camp with his weeping, for he
knew what would be required of all of them.

That captive girl lived with the tribe under the watch of the Wolf
man, the tribe's spiritual leader. She was given special lodging and
special food until everything was right for the sacrificial ceremony.
Until then, she lived among the tribe, probably not knowing what
was to come. I think Alice must have lain in the grass on summer
days watching the blue sky and clouds above her, listening to the
wind and the meadowlarks. She might have imagined herself that
captive girl living among the tribe. She might have closed her eyes
and seen everything—the songs, the dances, the passing of sacred
objects through smoke, the building of the scaffold—and felt it as
if it were her own body being painted, first red for a few days and
then, on the last day, half red, half black.

She must have felt confused as she was urged to mount the
scaffold, her willingness to go, without force, a testament to the
Wolf man's skills. She was captive to his songs, his threats, his stories. Not understanding, perhaps she felt a tinge of pride at being
at the center of the ritual. She must have felt a pinch as her hands
were tied with the sacred leather thongs to the center post of the

scaffold, and hearing the tribe singing, she would have looked out among them as they pressed against one another to get a glimpse of her.

By now, their faces would have become familiar to her. She would have noticed how all the men of the tribe, including the baby boys and the feeble elderly men, had brand new arrows for their bows. For just a minute, she must have been afraid, guessing perhaps what was to come, but before she could give in to her terror, one of those men ran quickly toward her with a lighted torch and pretended to touch her side. Still watching him run away, she barely noticed as another man, following close behind, expertly fitted an arrow into his bow and shot it into her side, piercing her heart so swiftly she felt nothing, only vaguely hearing, before her eyes closed, the roar of approval from the tribe.

I imagine how on one of those summer days Alice might have felt a sharp pain in her heart and awakened from her daydream. She wouldn't die that day, but her heart would be permanently damaged, leading to her death at the age of fifty-three when I was only two years old.

November 2001

RENOVATING A HOUSE requires intimacy with a building. By the time you've stripped wallpaper, pulled up carpets, removed cabinets, washed, sanded, and painted walls and woodwork, you know the lines and features of that house as you might the body of a lover. Our level of approaching intimacy with the country house, though, was less like that of a lover than like that of a forensic scientist. We would pull away the skin to reveal the bones, pry open the structure to expose its very bowels. And just as the coroner must be braced for the putrid, we knew we too would uncover things we might rather not find. Decay, rot, shoddy materials, insect infestations, and damage caused by rodents.

Ingrid had told us stories about the family who owned the house before she bought it. They'd lived like animals, she said, using the air ducts as garbage containers and creating a garbage heap outside the front door six feet high. The family's reputation in the surrounding area was so bad Ingrid had to work for years to convince local service providers to come out to the property.

Although we had concerns about what we would find as we began to gut this house, now that we were free to really look closely, we found the space more promising than we'd originally hoped. The kitchen as it now existed was 14 x 15. Since the new entrance would be moved from the kitchen to the living room, we would gain additional wall space for counters and cabinets. A bathroom/

laundry room off the kitchen seemed like wasted space, and we planned to recess a part of the kitchen to accommodate a large pantry cabinet and a built-in oven. Behind this recessed portion of the kitchen would be a small bathroom and adjacent to it a short hallway with just enough room at the end of it for the washer and dryer. In this way the kitchen would feel roomier, and we'd add another window for light. Once the bridge loan inspection was past and we could tear off the steel siding on the outside of the house, we would eventually add another door from the kitchen to the backyard, where we would build a porch leading onto a patio.

The living room and dining room, despite seeming cramped because of their decor, were in fact ample rooms. Combined into one room, the space would be 16 x 30. The second floor mirrored those dimensions. We planned one bedroom upstairs and a common area to be used for an office/library. While the upstairs felt spacious enough, knee walls limited the actual wall space.

Both downstairs bedrooms in the addition were roomy: 16 x 12 and 16 x 14. The bathroom in the addition was 8 x 10. The wide doorway leading into the addition was lower than regulation height and contributed to the current cave-like feeling of the addition. Noel would raise that doorway to a standard seven-foot opening, making the addition feel more intentional and one with the original house.

So now the work began. For several nights that first week after we took possession, three of the burly guys from the elevator, Rick, Tracy, and Rodney, followed Noel to the country house after their day's work and helped him demolish the walls of the living room and dining room. Rodney singlehandedly tore out one large section in the north wall. Together they also pulled up the carpets throughout the main floor of the house. When they'd finished, Noel and I scrutinized the red fir floors and concluded that, despite the ground-in dust and stubborn carpet backing, they would sand out well. Then the guys tore down the wall separating the living room and dining room. Noel had determined it wasn't a supporting wall, and he wouldn't need to build a header for it. The removal of that wall transformed the space even more than we'd hoped. Light flooded into the formerly dreary dining room. Now, however, a slope in the middle of the floor—caused by the weight of the old chimney Noel had removed—became apparent. In response to this, Noel set up jacks in the crawl space and over the next few weeks began to slowly raise that section of the floor.

Everything seemed to be going according to plan when we experienced an unexpected complication early in the month. We'd noticed the slight bulge on the south side of the house near the foundation when we first looked at the place, and Noel had known he'd likely encounter difficulties there; but he hadn't guessed the extent of the problem until the studs on that wall were fully exposed.

As the guys pulled away the trim board, it was clear the framing on the south side of the house had never been secured to the joists. Since the house was built, the studs had been slowly working away and askew from the joists, and that wall was now close to falling off the foundation.

I was at the American Literature Association conference in Washington, D.C., when Noel found the problem. He called me that night and didn't try to disguise his concern. It was a big challenge, and he wasn't sure he could take care of it on his own. We suddenly had to factor into our budget the possibility of hiring a block and beam crew to get the wall properly back onto the foundation. That night as I tried to sleep in a strange hotel, I had visions of the south wall of the house collapsing and our suddenly being the owners of a condemned property.

My initial response after 9/11 of flight from the city had long since been replaced with a more conservative desire for safety and shelter. This news from Noel about the precariousness of the house contributed to my growing regret over what I felt had been a hasty decision made during a stressful time.

When Noel called the next night, I could tell immediately he was feeling better. He, Rick, and Tracy had come upon a possible solution. Their plan involved bolting four-by-fours onto the exterior wall of the house near the foundation, under which they would place car jacks. Across the house and through the original exterior wall, they would stretch cables attached to come-alongs bolted into the concrete floor of the addition. It all sounded far-fetched to me, but I was encouraged by Noel's optimism and had no more dire images of the house collapsing as I fell asleep that night.

By the time I returned home, the guys had spent days working out the details of the plan and were feeling good about their progress. I was there watching on a peaceful fall day, as together—Tracy outside jacking and persuading with a sledgehammer, Noel working in the crawl space to keep the sill in line with the joists, and Rick winching the cables—they moved the wall back into place. Noel was anxious throughout the operation that the balloon framing might pop apart at the roof line, and he was openly relieved to see no evidence of this kind of damage as he tied the framing back to the joists with steel plates. After they'd finished, he was still grinning with relief when we all sat down to eat lunch together on the dusty living room floor and celebrated both their ingenuity and their hard work.

I knew this situation served as an illustration of what Noel would be facing almost daily on this project. Huge construction problems, all of them insurmountable to me, would have to be solved quickly and creatively. Emotionally, I was learning already to keep a distance from the day-to-day problems I had no ability to solve. I couldn't allow myself to fret as I had in D.C. Instead, Noel had to be able to talk to me, to think out loud, and my role had to be one of listening calmly. I knew I needed to be both involved in the situation and at an emotional remove.

We could hardly believe our good fortune as the mild weather continued, allowing Noel to tear off the old entry porch and frame in the new without fighting the cold. Our friend Bob Blomstrom came to help for the duration of that weekend project.

Only forty-five when he retired from farming, Bob and his wife, Theresa, had moved twenty years earlier to Lincoln, where they owned and managed rental properties. They'd done gut jobs on a couple of their rentals, so they understood what Noel was up against and would be a reassuring presence and an invaluable help in the months to come.

Bob had met Theresa while finishing a degree in art history at NYU. Born and raised in the Bronx, gorgeous Theresa had had many offers for marriage, but she was looking to get out of the life she seemed destined for, and Bob's proposal that they farm his family's property in Nebraska summers and travel winters was the winning one. Bob is a witty man, and he came to the house each morning with his thermos of coffee and a pickup full of tools, his eyes bright, wanting to talk about what he saw happening in the world, full of insights worth taking seriously.

Once Noel and Bob finished the new entryway, our temporary doorway consisted of two pieces of plywood on hinges that we kept secured at night with a clasp and a padlock. Flimsy closure, but it was what Noel felt would be best until we could put in the front door. Our new steps were wobbly cement blocks. Every muck bucket of debris we carried out of the house had to go out through this perilous passage as through the month we continued to demolish the upstairs, the kitchen, the bathrooms, and the bedrooms. Suddenly this small house of eighteen hundred square feet seemed huge, as bucket after bucket and truckload after truckload to the dump seemed to barely scratch the surface of what remained to be done.

In the midst of the worst of the demolition, only a few friends came to see the house. The debris created such thick dust we had to wear masks whenever we were inside, even if we weren't working.

Suzi, a friend and colleague from the University of Nebraska Press, where I worked, was one of those who came to see the house at this stage. She had a PhD in architectural history from Emory and was more interested than most people in the potential of buildings. I hoped she might have some suggestions for lighting, and she did. She stepped through and over the debris without flinching and squinted through the haze, her dust mask glowing in the gloom, to make suggestions, almost all of which I dutifully followed.

IN THE MIDDLE of the month, the Prairie Psychos—the band Noel played rhythm guitar with—had their debut Zoo bar gig. Noel had tried to counter my excitement about the show at Lincoln's legendary blues bar by reminding me they were the opening act, not the main attraction. The Psychos aren't a blues band, but for any musician in Lincoln, playing the Zoo is an incredible experience. In the heyday of jazz and blues, the Zoo was a regular stop on all the big tours, the bar where Jay McShann recorded his album Big Apple Bash in 1979. One of the stories surrounding the bar— many of them apocryphal I'm sure—has it that Charlie Parker got his nickname Yardbird when he hit and killed a chicken while on his way from Kansas City to Lincoln to play the Zoo.

The night of the gig was the first cold weather we'd had so far that autumn—a raw, windy night with temperatures near zero. Only our loyalty to Noel motivated Leif, Jordan, and me to leave the warmth and coziness of the pink house to go out. We'd plotted in advance how to get underage Jordan into the bar (Leif had turned twenty-one earlier that month) and had decided that if she went early with the band and helped them set up, she might be able to stay undetected to hear them play.

The Zoo is a small bar. The space is long and narrow, and the bar itself forms a corridor just inside the entrance. Unless you come early, it's standing room only in the small seating area and in the bottleneck along the bar itself. The stage is squeezed into the far end of the space, both bathrooms adjacent to it, so there is always a line of people beside the stage. An area the size of a large dining room table serves as a dance floor, and a few brave couples are always willing to try to dance there despite the restriction of their movements.

As the show was about to begin, Jordan and I were congratulating ourselves on the success of our little deception when suddenly sixteen-year-old Bronwyn materialized at our table. She'd had to work that night at the movie theater where she sold tickets, but, as she explained, when she got home at 9:00, she decided she wanted to hear the band.

I was flabbergasted. "But how did you get in?" She shrugged nonchalantly and casually took off her coat, all the while ignoring my gestures for her to hurry up and sit down so she wouldn't be spotted. "I just walked in," she told us after she finally sat down. During all the years I'd gone to hear bands at the Zoo bar, I'd never been allowed to simply walk past the doorman, but a number of times before, I'd observed Bronwyn's ability to throw back her shoulders and dare anyone to question her.

We ended our conversation quickly as the Psychos took the stage. To look at them, you'd assume they were a sedate group— three middle-aged men and a thirty-something—but the Psychos can rock, and an audience quickly forgets appearances. Scott, the lead singer and bass player, writes most of their songs. His wife, Barb, estimated at that time he'd written at least five hundred songs. Those who know Scott feel strongly that someday—after he dies perhaps—the world will discover a great hidden talent, but he's not ambitious for himself in that way and is content to play and record on a small scale. By day he's an English professor at Nebraska Wesleyan University. Larry, who plays a tasty lead guitar, is also an English professor at Nebraska Wesleyan. The band has had a series of drummers, but that night it was John T., a graduate student at the University of Nebraska.

The Psychos' debut at the Zoo was a great success, and we left the bar and faced the cold of that night still warmed by the congratulations of those who'd come to hear them play. The band was important to Noel, and its weekly rehearsals (what all the guys referred to as their alternative to poker night) were the one thing I felt certain he wouldn't interrupt even for the house project.

SOMETIMES ON WEEKEND days Noel took short breaks from his work at the house, and we walked together the length of the property. During these walks we became acquainted with the high meadow to the west and the peaceful grove of trees in the northwest corner of the place. In one of those old trees were the remains of a long abandoned tree house. A rusting car hidden in the trees never failed to fascinate Finnegan, who on every walk with us jumped first into the car's open trunk and then into the rotting back seat, eagerly rooting out the mice nesting there.

The southern half of the property was in a flood plain: a mixture of brome grass, tall swamp grass, goldenrod, native grasses, Osage orange, and red cedar trees interspersed with a few elms, diamond willows, hackberries, locusts, and cottonwoods.

Although we never spotted any deer during these walks, we saw evidence of their nests everywhere in this south section. And indeed, our neighbors Mark and Linda had told us how every night they watched from their house as a herd of ten or twelve jumped the fence onto our property.

At night, away from the lights of the city, the dark sky was filled with stars. Every night, no matter its stage, the moon was magnificent. One evening in particular as we were about to leave the house, we watched a thick mist rise and settle in the trees across the road from us while above it the stars shone in a clear sky. The coyotes were out that night, yipping and howling in the distance, their eerie cries echoing across the silent hills.

A few nights later Noel came home to tell me about a scare he'd had while covering the debris in the back of the truck after that evening's demolition. He was tired that night around 10:00 when he heard someone yelling behind the barn. Then another yell and another. It sounded like a gang of kids, and Noel couldn't imagine what they might be up to. He confessed he felt a little threatened by it. I see him there scoping out the distance between himself and them, laying his hands on the crowbar or some other tool he might use as a weapon if needed. The yelling started again, only this time one of the yells became a yip and then a howl. Soon the whole pack was howling. Noel laughed at himself with relief when he realized he'd mistaken coyotes for kids.

It was on one of those cold November nights that the sales rep from Pella Windows drove out and measured the house for new doors and windows. We needed these measurements for the framing, but it would be a long time before new doors and windows could be installed. Unfortunately, because the siding on the house was steel and everything had to be painted and sided to pass the inspection for the permanent loan, we had to postpone placing the new windows themselves until after the inspection, at which time we would pull off the old siding and replace it with new board. Once again, the need to pass an inspection before we locked into the permanent loan meant we had to do extra work now. We planned to enlarge most of the windows and to add new doors. Noel would need to frame for those changes in advance, even though that framing would be temporarily covered by drywall until after the inspection.

AS MUCH AS NOEL begrudged having to interrupt work for any reason, the calendar doesn't stop for projects, and Thanksgiving came as it always does. Since Bronwyn had to work later that afternoon, the girls drove out in a separate car to my mother's house in nearby Ceresco, giving Noel and me the rare opportunity to spend time alone with Leif.

Leif is a quiet man, modest and soft-spoken. Lately, he had seemed even more reserved than usual, and I made a decision as we waited for Noel to fill the car with gas.

"Leif," I said. "I need you to reassure me you're happy."

He hesitated for a moment before finally saying, "I'm not *always* happy."

It was risky, and I knew it, but I pressed on anyway waiting only for Noel to get into the car before saying as we pulled into traffic, "I'm only going to say this one time, and then I'll never mention it again. If any of your unhappiness has to do with getting married, I hope you'll really think about it." I paused. "Who you marry will determine the course of your life."

Leif nodded thoughtfully. I wasn't surprised by his reaction. He isn't one to strike out defensively. But I couldn't be sure what he was thinking either, and I knew it would be counterproductive to pry. If, however, I'd known what was facing him with my family that day, I wouldn't have said anything in the first place.

Almost from the minute we arrived until we said our goodbyes hours later, my two brothers, Cam and Tad, along with my brother-in-law Kent, gave Leif no end of flak about his engagement. Like me, all of them had married young and had regrets about it. Fortunately, they're all funny men and clearly fond of Leif, so their concerns were couched in good humor. Still, Leif couldn't have missed the point when as we were leaving; his Uncle Kent made a gesture of hara-kari.

I apologized for their behavior as we drove away, but once again,

Leif was philosophical. "It's okay. They're just trying to protect me." As much as I was relieved he hadn't taken offense, I was concerned by what Leif's tepid response to such emotionally charged criticism might really mean.

We didn't talk about it further as we drove to Omaha that evening to pick up Noel's parents, Floyd and Marie. They were coming from southern California to stay the long weekend, their bags packed with work clothes and long johns, ready to help us with demolition during part of their stay.

Seventh-day Adventist religious practice forbids its members to work from sundown on Friday until sundown on Saturday, so we all took advantage of their beliefs to rest the day after Thanksgiving. Although Noel was raised in the church and attended Seventh-day Adventist schools his entire life, he was never devout, and shortly after he left home, he left the church. I'm sure his parents were at first alarmed by his decision to marry a divorced woman with three children, but in the years since our marriage they'd been nothing but generous to us.

Sunday was a jarring contrast to the coziness of the day before as we drove to the frigid country house to continue demolition. Marie, the girls, and I all tackled the kitchen walls, while Noel, Floyd, and Leif removed the kitchen cabinets and all the old light fixtures throughout the house. Marie seemed enthusiastic about the work of knocking down old plaster, swinging a claw hammer a bit wildly at times as she balanced on one leg on the high rung of a ladder, one foot kicked back daintily. Noel stopped on one of his trips through the room and laughed while admonishing her to be careful. Marie had seemed confused for a moment by his comment, apparently oblivious to her posture in her intensity of focus. Bronwyn, too, liked the satisfaction of dismantling walls. At one point she exclaimed, "This is so much fun!" as she brought down the crowbar with a flourish.

When we left that night, all that remained to be removed in the kitchen were the linoleum, the trim around the doors and windows, and the plaster on the ceiling. We were cold and exhausted on the drive back to Lincoln, but we were happy too. His parents' support meant a lot to Noel. Until that day they hadn't seen the house or had any sense of the scope of what we were facing. Seeing now the enormity of the project, Floyd was already making plans for several return trips. He'd recently retired from a career with the airlines and could fly free.

Even the small amount of time I spent helping with the demolition had given me a healthy respect for the backbreaking work Noel was doing night after night. In addition to the inherently hard work of demolition, he'd developed severe tendinitis in his right elbow after a few days of repetitively swinging a crowbar. If it had been me, the project would have come to a complete stop, but Noel responded with his usual stoicism. "When I finish demolition, the pain will stop." There was nothing to be done, he reassured me, but to keep going.

During the last remaining days of November, after Floyd and Marie left and while Noel continued demolition, I made it my project to pull up the linoleum covering the kitchen floor. From the beginning we'd been reminding ourselves the original wood floors might not be adequate, but in truth we were counting on their soundness. So I began the job with optimism.

Unfortunately, my labor that day revealed one problem after another: deep gouges in the wood, large oil stains, and dry rot. I finally called Noel into the room to show him the extent of the damage. It was clear to both of us the floor would have to be removed or covered. Another cost to factor into the budget, another task to add to Noel's already crushing list of things to do. But even worse was the question of what to use in its place. The idea of new wood flooring against old wood set Noel's teeth on edge. Ceramic tile, another serious option, seemed out of place in the kitchen of this house. Plus, Noel had concerns about whether he could in fact make the subflooring stable enough to support tile. He eventually added a steel beam to reinforce the joists under the kitchen floor, in case tile became our best option.

Since we already knew we had to replace a few boards in the living room floor and to lay new flooring in the entire 3 x 15 section to the west of the upstairs landing, I started asking around about a large quantity—over six hundred square feet—of salvage fir flooring. None of the salvage businesses in Lincoln had that much fir flooring available. Finally, a friend who'd recently restored a Victorian house mentioned Bob Cox in the little town of Newman Grove, a two-hour drive northwest of Lincoln.

When I finally reached Bob Cox by phone, he said he was *pretty* sure he had enough fir flooring for us. He was an older man, retired from farming, and his noncommittal response didn't inspire confidence. I asked if there was any way he could check to be sure. "No," he said. "But I'm *pretty* sure I'll have what you need. Just let me know when you're coming."

Among my many feelings about this project was my revulsion at the idea of having to make it a cookie-cutter house because we didn't have adequate time to search for what we wanted. I knew that in our haste to finish on time it would be a temptation to buy materials quickly. Buying through salvage operations is not speedy. Now, in addition to the usual time-intensive nature of a purchase of this sort, we'd need to add a four-hour round-trip drive, with little confidence about finding on the other end what we needed from an eccentric old man.

With each passing week, we'd become more aware of the scale of the project. Already in November we knew we couldn't finish the work under deadline without the help and sacrifice of our friends and family. Our need for such help was humbling, and we often felt ashamed of the burden we'd made of ourselves for those who loved us.

The Parsonage
LITCHFIELD, NEBRASKA, 1967–1968

WHEN SHE WAS TWELVE, my mother started attending the little Christian Church (Church of Christ) in Litchfield, riding into town each week with a neighboring farmer. Mom once told me her family (non-church-going folk) gave her a hard time about her decision. They couldn't understand her devotion. But then maybe they hadn't heard Gail D. preach. He was handsome and charismatic. He and his vivacious wife had just been hired by the church. He was smart and sophisticated; he told stories and quoted scripture; he must have made the world come alive. Unaccustomed as she was to eloquence, my mother would have been captivated. Later, when he abandoned his wife for another woman in the congregation and left his ministry in the spectacularly public way that is possible only in small and insular communities, my mother never seemed to have let her disappointment in him interfere with her faith. Whenever she saw Gail D. infrequently in the years to come, I never heard her say a bad word about him. He still held for her some of the charisma he had when she was a young girl, and she retained her admiration for him and for his influence in the life of faith she had found in her adolescence.

She married my father knowing he was not a believer, and I don't think she intended to convert him. She attended church alone with the four of us, as far as I know not pressuring Dad to join her. It was only later as we grew older that he began to accompany us more and more until finally he met, in that same small church where my mother had become a convert, yet another charismatic minister, and he also became a changed person.

The Christian Church was founded in the early part of the nineteenth century by brothers Alexander and Thomas Campbell, immigrants to the U.S. from Ireland. Originally calling themselves Campbellites, Alexander Campbell initiated reforms advocating a return to what he called "simplicity of faith," following Scripture rather than church tradition. He believed church hierarchy and centralized governance had led contemporary believers far from the roots of the primitive church and the first-century Christians.

These principles still define the denomination today. Characterized by extreme congregational autonomy, each congregation elects its own leaders (elders and deacons chosen from the laity), hires and fires its own ministers, and makes autonomous decisions without the oversight of a general conference or denominational headquarters. Three branches of the denomination now exist: Non-Instrumental, in which use of any musical instrument in worship service is considered in violation of Scripture (this branch split from the original group in 1910); Independent, the central branch of the denomination, which, like the Non-Instrumentalists, believes in the infallibility of Scripture, closed communion, baptism by immersion for salvation but allows the use of musical instruments in the worship service; and finally Disciples of Christ, the liberal expression of the denomination: they are members of the World Council of Churches, accept open communion—allowing all believers, no matter the form of their baptism, to partake—and question the infallibility of Scripture (this branch split from the original church in 1960). My family belonged to the Independent Christian Church.

When I was ten, the minister at the Christian Church in Litchfield left for another ministry, and the church elders, including my father, began to fill in for him on Sundays, taking turns preaching for Sunday morning services. My father was a shy man, not a talker by nature. Nor was he particularly literate, but he worked hard on those sermons and began to build a small library of reference books and Bible commentaries to supplement his knowledge of scripture. I remember him earnestly writing drafts of his sermons at the kitchen table and asking Mom to read and edit them for grammar and organization.

At the time the minister's family left, our family was asked to move into the parsonage. A two-story stucco, the parsonage sat on a large shady lot in the middle of Litchfield, only a block off Main Street and behind the town mortuary. My favorite room in the house was the dining room with its bay window, hardwood floor, and huge claw-foot walnut dining table—a table left behind when the minister's family moved away. My piano was in this room, and I liked how the sound echoed against the room's high ceiling.

A small living room adjoined the dining room and served mainly to showcase the new color TV Dad had bought earlier that year in Broken Bow. We'd seen it through the windows of the hardware store one cold winter night, amidst washing machines, kitchen stoves, and stereos. The four of us kids had stopped on the street mesmerized by an episode of *Bat Man*, the text sound effects—"pow," "bam," "crash"—in bursts of bright colors we'd never imagined when watching the program on our old black and white television.

The upstairs bedroom I shared with my sister in the parsonage had three squatty windows beneath the gabled roof, and the walls bore the lines of the house's Victorian-era architecture, including knee walls in part of the room. I was reading Nancy Drew mysteries at the time and spent many happy hours reading in this room, often going to bed with a flashlight so I wouldn't have to quit reading once the lights were supposed to be out.

I got my books from the Litchfield library. No larger than our dining room, the library was located on Main Street in a flat-roofed, one-room, brick building a couple of blocks away from the parsonage. The library's wood floor creaked in the silent room where I was often the only patron browsing the shelves. Staffed by volunteers, the library was open only a few hours a week. I liked it best in winter when the heady smell of the propane used to heat the room mingled with the smell of dusty shelves and old books. This smell, combined with my excitement in the presence of so many books, created a kind of altered state. The titles for kids were located on one bottom shelf along the north wall. Once I'd exhausted all the Nancy Drew mysteries, I turned to what I came to think of as the suffering animal stories: *Black Beauty, Savage Sam, Old Yeller,* and many others of that ilk. Already sensitive about animals, I cried myself to sleep many nights worrying about all the mistreated animals in the world.

I'D BEEN BAPTIZED WHEN I was six years old during a week of revival at which a missionary from Africa spoke to the congregation. For that whole week our family had driven into town from the farm for the nightly sermons. For some reason this missionary noticed me at age six and was kind to me. I was impressed with his talks, with the exciting places he described. I may have been as attracted to the Christian life for the promise of seeing those faraway places as I was for any belief in God at that time. After each night's talk, I went into the church foyer, where the missionary had set up tables displaying artifacts of the African people among whom he lived. Bowls, pipes, figures carved in stone or wood, and photographs of the people themselves. I'd never seen a black person.

Now that my father was the interim minister, we were more involved in revival meetings of this sort and other events at the church. Many traveling ministries came through our town in the late 1960s while we lived in the parsonage. One revival favorite was a man who simultaneously made chalk drawings as he preached.

Each night, he finished his drawing at the same time he finished his talk. The lights of the sanctuary were dimmed, and a black light illuminated the drawing. The congregation always gasped in amazement as they suddenly saw the face of Jesus, or the scene of Golgotha, or Jesus ascending into the heavens, where before they'd seen only abstract images.

Yet another speaker was an older man distinguished among Nebraska Church of Christ members as a biblical scholar, who'd made his life's study the Temple in Jerusalem. He traveled with a scale model he'd made of the Temple, according to the biblical speculations in the book of Genesis. He took this model with him from church to church and talked about the uses and the symbolic meanings of each aspect of the building. I tried to be interested in these talks, but I was always disappointed by the smallness, the downright plainness of the Temple. I wanted it to be grand. I'd always imagined it should be grand.

Dad still owned the gas station. That first winter we lived in the parsonage produced a major blizzard. When we came home from school early one day, kicking the snow from our boots and shaking it from our hats and scarves on the front porch, we smelled delicious aromas that meant someone had been baking. Inside, the kitchen counters were covered with loaves of fresh bread and cinnamon rolls. Highway 2 was closed, so Dad had come home early to bake. While we listened to the gale outside and watched the snow drift against the bay windows in the dining room, we ate warm cinnamon rolls snug in the warmth of home. Other dads we knew didn't bake, but our dad had always been different.

When the storm had still not subsided by Sunday morning, the rarest of rare events occurred: church services were canceled. Dad decided we'd have church at home. After breakfast, while the dishes were being cleared, I played a few hymns on the piano and waited for the family to gather at the claw-foot table. Before our little home service could start, Mom jumped up from the table.

She returned in a few minutes having added to her T-shirt and jeans a pillbox hat, matching heels, and a purse. We kids were delighted, but Dad—who was usually charmed by my mother's antics—didn't seem to think her attempt at humor was very funny. I was disappointed and a little nervous when he didn't laugh and go along with her teasing as usual, but instead scolded, "It's time to be serious now, Elaine."

In the large basement of the parsonage was a long concrete tunnel leading to a root cellar. My friends and I liked to pretend this was our civil defense shelter. It was 1968, a time when some people in the U.S. were talking about storing extra food, exchanging their money for gold blocks, preparing for the worst—the communist threat. At school, civil defense drills instructed us to hide under our desks or go to areas considered safe in the building in "case of a national emergency." Yellow and black civil defense signs indicated where the shelters were. What was meant by national emergency was never made clear to us; nor was it clear how our flimsy desks would protect us from harm. We were simply expected to do as we were told. Still, we welcomed the disruption of these civil defense drills in the midst of a school day. We felt a sort of thrill at the idea of unseen danger around us.

For a few church people at that time, "national emergency" was synonymous with the apocalypse, which scripture told us would signal the second coming of Christ. They believed communists would act as the tools of the anti-Christ.

That year I went to Bible camp for the first time at Pibel Lake in the Sandhills: Pibel Bible Camp. There, a young minister from Ord, Nebraska, J. H. Schroeder, would be my first encounter with this survivalist movement. He wore ranch-style western clothes on his tall thin frame. He took himself very seriously, and his intense personality made him an easy target for teasing. I once watched him bow his head and cry while being harassed by fifth-grade campers during the lunch hour. He was an advocate of preparing for the hard times ahead and in a remote hillside had built an underground shelter that he'd stocked with canned goods and water, planning for those days when Satan would be set loose in the world.

These were the years when at church camp or at revival meetings I first began to hear the testimonies of recent converts to the faith, people who, like my father, told about a life lived badly in the world and the moment when they saw the light and turned to Jesus. Unlike my father's story, though, which seemed to focus more on a darkness of the heart, these converts were often former drug addicts or recovering alcoholics, people running from one dramatically failed life or another. Mostly men. I could never seem to get enough of their stories, though without fail I liked best the details of their troubled previous lives better than the saintly lives they claimed they were now living.

AFTER OUR MOVE TO the parsonage, I no longer needed to be supervised crossing Highway 2 and the railroad tracks, so I saw my friend Rhonda every day. Rhonda loved horses, and her room was filled with plastic models of every breed she could find. She owned a black Shetland pony named Tar Baby she kept in a corral on the west edge of town, and we trained that ill-natured little horse to let us ride double, taking him into the fields on the outskirts of town, with Rhonda's basset hound in tow, to go "rabbit hunting."

Together we also explored the many empty buildings and houses in Litchfield. At one time, almost a century earlier, it had been a larger town with two newspapers, two grocery stores, several restaurants, and a doctor's office. One of the old newspaper offices sat empty and locked on Main Street, which didn't stop us from getting inside through a window in the back. There we discovered an ancient press and, sitting on a counter in the middle of the floor, a strange typewriter with long metal fingers sticking up from it.

Yellowed newspapers lay stacked against the walls. The building seemed to have been left hastily in the middle of a day of business. The most memorable empty house we discovered had been severely damaged by a fire on the first floor. We thought nothing of walking past the charred walls and burned floorboards to climb to the second story, where, like the newspaper office, we found bedrooms left just as they'd been when their occupants fled, obviously in a hurry. In one room was a chest holding what looked like party dresses; a few bureaus had been abandoned with their drawers pulled open, empty except for a few stray photographs, scarves, and purses.

One day a county deputy sheriff interrupted us in that house. We heard his footsteps on the floor below and froze, at first thinking he was a ghost. A ghost seemed more likely than a deputy sheriff in little Litchfield, Nebraska, but when he called up to us— "Hey, you girls. Girls!"—we slowly crept to the top of the stairs and peered at him. He beckoned us downstairs. "You need to get out of here. This house is condemned." I'd never heard of a house being condemned. I'd only heard of people being condemned—to hell. Once we were outside, he made us listen as he lectured us about the risks of going into empty houses: " . . . beams falling . . . floors giving way . . . stairs collapsing." As he talked, we were already far away, plotting our next adventure. His cautions were mere yammering. We were confident nothing could ever hurt us.

We were puzzled though as to why, at some point in the past, people had left so suddenly. I would learn later that a number of dramatic exoduses from Nebraska had occurred since it achieved statehood in 1867. In 1874, in the midst of a year of terrible drought, a plague of locusts infested the state. Dead locusts piled like snow drifts, bringing trains to a halt because of the carnage on the tracks and leading many homesteaders to conclude the state was uninhabitable. Those who stayed experienced the economic boom of the 1880s, a decade when the towns in Nebraska flourished and hopes for the future of the state soared. However, those flush days came to an end during a long period of devastating drought from 1893 to 1896, after which the state experienced a second mass exodus. By the time drought again struck the state in the mid-1930s, exacerbating the economic devastation caused by the nationwide depression, optimistic state promotion had come to an end, and towns in rural Nebraska never fully recovered.

Rhonda's family lived in a formerly elegant house built by old Doc Redburg, a man still talked about in town as though he lived just around the corner, when in fact he'd been dead for many years. He'd been the town's last doctor. Rhonda's house, though now a bit shabby and cluttered, still harbored evidence of its illustrious past life: oak floors and pillars, built-in bookcases and buffets, a grand staircase, an impressive mirrored hall valet, spacious, high-ceilinged rooms, beveled glass windows, and several sets of French doors. In the large yard, now weedy and overgrown, was an empty, concrete-lined fishpond with a tiny concrete bridge. Beside the pond was a large, clear, aquamarine stone the size of a television.

Rhonda's mother was divorced. She'd moved with her five children from upstate New York a few years before Rhonda and I became friends. Three of Rhonda's siblings were much older than she was. One sister, Chris, a high school cheerleader, taught Rhonda and me how to do the newest dances: the jerk and the spider. Another sister, Kathy, was a student at Kearney State College. She came home occasionally on weekends like foreign royalty, her glamorous straight black hair parted in the middle, her eyebrows penciled into thin arches, her pouty mouth painted with white lipstick. While home, she did little I could see except smoke cigarettes and nap on the couch. Rhonda's brother, Del, was in junior high. He invented and built exotic hybrid bicycles and other carnivalesque contraptions. He tinkered constantly with the motor of a junk car stalled in their garage. Del often grew irritated with Rhonda and me. We always hoped he would. If we were lucky, he'd leave his tinkering and chase us around the yard while we shrieked and ran. If we were unlucky, he caught us. Dell was a big boy, tall and husky for his age, and he easily held us together between his feet where he grabbed each of us roughly by one ear and banged our heads together.

When I went home with Rhonda after school, we usually found her mother sitting in the kitchen in her pajamas, having just woken up after working her night job at a factory in Kearney, her children talking to her at the table while she smoked and ate breakfast. Sometimes Rhonda's elderly grandmother traveled on a Greyhound bus the twenty miles from Ravenna to visit. Each time, she stayed several days. Her thin white hair stood on end; she wore her robe and slippers all day and padded from room to room fussing about the kids, who affectionately ignored her. She hated to climb the stairs to the bathroom and muttered complaints to herself, until at some point she would abruptly stand up and announce to the room, "I can't forget about it anymore," before she shuffled up the grand staircase to the bathroom.

In Rhonda's house was a great mystery that took up much of our imaginative energy the year and a half I lived in the parsonage. The family had rented the house from Doc Redburg's relatives with the stipulation they could use every room except one closet, which was to remain locked. This closet was located in what was then Rhonda's bedroom but had earlier been her sister Chris's room. The landlord had offered no explanation for this exclusion to the rental deal, and the inscrutability of it caused a great deal of speculation between Rhonda and me. No doubt knowing of our obsession, Del and Chris told us how one night during a terrible thunderstorm, when the room had still been Chris's, the closet door was blown open to reveal a shredded window shade. They hinted someone had once been trapped there and had been desperate to escape. There were objects covered by sheets, they told us, among which they implied there might even have been a body. Beneath the door they found two dark red drops on the floor. After the storm, Chris claimed, she'd taken a sample to her high school chemistry lab, where the teacher determined it was, in fact, human blood. Rhonda and I were wild with the terror and elation of what that closet might be hiding.

I wanted to be a member of Rhonda's family. Even with its problems, I was attracted to their energy and creativity, adventurousness and freedom. By comparison, my family felt boring and restrictive. My whereabouts were closely monitored. Our house had to be kept tidy. I couldn't stay up late or go downtown on Saturday nights when the grocery store and the bar and cafe stayed open and people from nearby farms came in to do their shopping. Instead, I listened with envy from my open bedroom window on summer Saturday nights to the sounds of car doors slamming and people talking on Main Street. How I longed to be out among them. I took my disappointment to the pages of my latest Nancy Drew book and lost myself in her freedom to come and go. Nancy could go anywhere. She neither asked for nor needed permission to leave.

I'd begun to sense a wider world beyond our little town. The threat of unseen enemies—both those that threatened the country and those that threatened my soul—captivated me. Like those former inhabitants of Nebraska who'd left everything behind in their hurry to leave the state, like Rhonda's sophisticated older siblings, like Nancy Drew who came and went with perfect freedom as she solved mysteries, like the missionaries I met who'd sought out faraway and exotic places, I longed for adventure. I had no idea how soon my family would embark on its own adventure or what a disappointment it would prove to be.

December 2001

I WAS TRAVELING FOR WORK again when there was more bad news. Noel didn't say anything right away about his mishap when he called me in New York early in December, but before hanging up, he casually mentioned he'd fallen down the basement stairs at the country house. He hadn't been hurt badly when his foot slipped between the narrow stair treads and sent him tumbling, but it seemed miraculous he hadn't broken a leg or suffered a head injury. For weeks, I'd been imagining the possibility of him getting hurt while working alone on the country place and had been feeling we needed to get a cell phone, something we'd resisted before this. Now with news of his fall, I made getting a phone a priority on my to-do list when I got home.

After my return, Bob and Theresa came out to help us finish pulling up the carpets in the upstairs. They brought with them tools for demolition. When Theresa is in work mode, there's no small talk; and as soon as they arrived, she was ready to start. Her daughters tease that she has only two speeds: fast and faster. That was fine with Noel and me.

After we finished with the carpets, Theresa and I pulled all the nails protruding from the studs both upstairs and down, while Noel and Bob finished the demolition in the addition. At last, five weeks after we'd begun, the demolition was complete. The weather was mild enough for us to sit outside and eat our lunch.

Other than fighting the wind, we were comfortable in light jackets. As we ate, I looked with fondness at Bob and Theresa. They'd been good friends for almost twenty years. Theresa is tall and broad shouldered. She walks with long, athletic strides and at sixty was still a handsome woman. Her impoverished and painful childhood in the Bronx made her the most pragmatic and unsentimental person I knew. I hadn't always gotten the answers I wanted from Theresa, but she always told me the truth. And I'd been wise enough in the past to listen closely to her advice.

I first met her in a comparative religion class at the university. I'm attracted to confident older women, and Theresa is such a woman. I'd been shy about meeting her, and it wasn't until the last few weeks of class when by chance we sat together that we struck up a lasting friendship. I was eight-and-a-half months pregnant with Bronwyn at the time, planning to give birth at home with the aid of a midwife, and Theresa was interested in the home birth and the baby. She and Bob left for Italy at the end of the semester, and she sent me a postcard while they were away. Later, she brought a gift to the house for newborn Bronwyn. It was the beginning of the most influential friendship of my life.

Theresa's influence was profound a few years later when I made a volatile change in my life, leaving a fundamentalist Christian worldview. She has no patience for the language of martyrdom and is downright allergic to women sacrificing themselves to anything, especially church doctrine. Hers was a powerful voice raised against the voices of the faithful when I was struggling to leave my husband. I had three small children and no visible means of support at the time, but Theresa and Bob stood beside me through that seismic shift and, along with my parents, provided emotional support through the long and bitter divorce and custody battle. When they first met Noel, they took to him immediately. Through the years, he'd become almost a son to them, and it was very clear to me as I watched all of them that day, they were helping him now as he had helped them for years with their rental properties.

That December day happened to be my forty-fourth birthday. It seemed not all that long ago I'd faced myself in the mirror on my thirty-third birthday, a devastated woman: homeless, jobless, only halfway through a master's degree in English, unsure if I would win the fight to keep my children. I'd seen myself clearly in the mirror that day eleven years earlier and, despite the dire circumstances of my life at that time, had made a promise to myself that in ten years I would have come so far I wouldn't recognize myself. I remembered now the promise I'd made and wondered a bit at the confidence of my younger self despite everything to the contrary.

NOW THAT THE DEMOLITION was finished and the house swept as clean as possible, Noel put in new air ducts. It was cold, dirty, miserable work for him as he hunkered for hours at a time in the dark three-foot-high crawl space under the living room. I was there to help part of the time, handing down tools, holding ducts in place as he nailed from below. When he wanted a tool, he reached a hand up through a hole in the living room floor. More than once I was caught off guard by that disembodied hand waving in the middle of the room.

Although the month had started out unseasonably mild, the weather began to grow cold again. From the beginning Noel's plan to finish framing before running the electrical wires and adding insulation had seemed like a bad idea to Bob, who was worried about the quickly dropping outside temperatures and Noel having to work in a frigid house.

Given his concern, perhaps it shouldn't have surprised us when Bob approached Noel in mid-December with an offer to do the wiring for him. To Noel's protests that the framing wouldn't be finished, Bob answered, "You don't have to have every framing board in place to wire." Although it was technically true, Noel still felt it wasn't the best way to do things.

I was listening to bits of their conversation and couldn't help noticing how they both spoke in the halting, awkward way people do when they're trying not to offend one another. Bob was right to be concerned about the cold, while Noel, a perfectionist in some ways, was suddenly feeling a loss of control over an already unwieldy project.

I wisely stayed out of the conversation, knowing they'd have to work it out between themselves. Noel made it clear he didn't want to take advantage of Bob. Bob wouldn't hear of it and went on to say that Cathy (his and Theresa's oldest daughter) would be back in Nebraska for three weeks over the Christmas break. She'd mentioned one of the things she wanted to do during that time was the wiring in the country house for us.

"You've done a lot for us over the years with our rentals," Bob finally insisted. "Cathy and I really want to help." At this, Noel reluctantly gave in.

Before Cathy was due to arrive, I was enlisted to help Bob run the wires through the house and mark where to locate outlets, light switches, and the light fixtures in every room except the kitchen. I was thankful then for my colleague Suzi's earlier visit in November. Because of her advice, I had a clear idea of what I wanted for lighting. Noel raced frantically to get as much as possible framed in advance of us.

In addition to assisting Bob with the preliminary wiring, preparing for Christmas, and celebrating Bronwyn's seventeenth birthday, my big responsibility for the month of December was to come up with a kitchen layout by the time Cathy and Bob started to run wires in the kitchen. It was essential for them to know where I wanted cabinets, appliances, lights, and outlets.

The first cabinet company I worked with early in December had given me a tentative plan, but I couldn't find cabinets I liked in their more affordable lines. I next tried the economy route, checking out Home Depot and Menards. My efforts there all ended in frustration. At one point I waited for an hour at Menards for someone to talk to me before I finally gave up. The young man at Home Depot was helpful in plotting out a provisional kitchen plan on their computer, but when I got it back to the house, it was four inches too short on the south side. Call after call in an attempt to revise the plan ended nowhere. I realized then if I had this much trouble correcting the plan, we'd be in big trouble at the point of installation resolving any problems with the cabinets themselves. Before her arrival in Nebraska, Cathy called to suggest we look into IKEA cabinets, but we concluded, after adding up the total cost with the shipping charges, we'd be ahead to work with an established cabinet company in Lincoln.

Despite all this effort, I still didn't have a definite plan in place when, before Christmas, Cathy and her husband, Rick, returned to Nebraska. We hadn't seen them since before September 11th. Although their home in Morningside Heights was far from lower Manhattan, Rick had been the acting building commissioner for Manhattan at the time the towers fell. He'd slept on a cot at Ground Zero after the attack, being awakened numerous times during those first nights to check the stability of buildings in the surrounding area. We knew he'd seen the inside of hell during the past few months.

Cathy, like Rick, is an engineer. She's a petite, pretty woman, who despite her pixyish appearance is one of the two most formidable women I know. After long observation, I've concluded it's in part because she doesn't smile easily. I believe it's likely she adopted this trait when trying to establish herself in a male-dominated career where her looks were potentially detrimental.

She's a capable woman and during her summers in Nebraska had restored the Victorian house they owned in the Near South neighborhood. We all felt things speed up once Cathy was on the job, energetic and efficient.

Rick helped Noel finish the framing and hang insulation on the ceiling of the second floor. A former Nebraska football player, Rick's a strong man and was often called upon by the Blomstroms to perform the hard physical labor on their various rental properties. In this project, especially in light of the past few months, we wanted to spare him that role.

As Christmas drew nearer without a plan for the kitchen layout, everyone involved began to lose patience with me. Much of the delay, I insisted, was caused by our uncertainty about the kitchen appliances. Through November and now well into December, whenever we had a few extra minutes, Noel and I continued to narrow our options. During the week I went to the library to check consumer reports about the various brands we'd seen in the stores. The kitchen appliances represented a major purchase and something we would have to live with for a long time, so I didn't want to make a hasty decision.

The appliances I wanted were all over budget, and I'd lain awake one night early in the month worrying that if I simply bought what we could afford, I wouldn't like the kitchen in this house as much as the one in the pink house. Around this time, one of my colleagues in Massachusetts, upon hearing the story of our house renovation through e-mail, had responded to some of my anxieties about the move with the statement, "At least you'll be moving into your dream house"—to which I had petulantly responded, "I live in my dream house. I'm moving into a house I don't yet recognize." I wasn't proud of my whining, but I still wasn't sure this would be a good change in my life.

Not long after this, I awoke one morning with a resolution and told Noel I wanted to use some of the money my grandmother left me to make the kitchen in the country house better than the kitchen I loved in the pink house. With the stock market plummeting daily, most people would have argued it was a lunatic time to sell investments, but those same people would likely have said it was a lunatic time to be doing any of this at all. Why suddenly try to be cautious and logical, I reasoned, when we'd clearly embarked on this scheme and needed to see it through.

Even though I felt I was working feverishly to finalize the kitchen plan, it wasn't fast enough. One evening shortly before Christmas, Noel and I went to Cathy and Rick's Lincoln home for dinner. The house was cozy that night as we sat around their dining room table to look at what I had so far. I hoped it might be adequate for them to get started with the wiring, but apparently it wasn't. Both Cathy and Noel were gentle but obviously frustrated with my obtuseness. It was clear to me how desperate Cathy was that night when she pulled out the IKEA catalog and began to run a few numbers. She volunteered to do all the figuring for the cabinets if I would just make a decision about the appliances, so we could at least have something more concrete to work with.

I definitely wanted to have a part in making these decisions, but I wasn't sure I liked having to make so many of the decisions alone. I felt isolated that night. In the economy of home restoration, my skills as a publisher seemed frivolous; my knowledge, esoteric frippery. And now, because of my seeming inability to focus or follow through with a plan for the kitchen, I appeared not only inept but lazy as well.

Chagrined, I met with Lori, a salesperson at Lincoln Cabinet, the next morning, telling her I needed a final plan as soon as possible. By now, I had a pretty clear idea about the appliances I wanted and a good sense of how I wanted the kitchen to look. Within a few hours, Lori had drawn up the final plan.

At last, everyone was happy, and the tension broke. The next day while Cathy and Bob wired and Noel framed in the unheated, uninsulated house, outside temperatures fell below zero. Together, Rick and I drove through the frigid, snowy Nebraska countryside to Ernie's Store in the little town of Ceresco to order the appliances. Despite being bundled in numerous layers, stocking caps, long johns, and thick gloves, our teeth chattered until at last the car's heater kicked in. Our clothes steamed, and the windows fogged as we started to thaw out.

TO THIS POINT ON THE PROJECT, if I was often supportive, I was equally—if not more—often frightened, frustrated, still ambivalent. Noel's energies, as I had predicted in September, had quickly shifted to the new house. Working there forty to fifty hours a week hadn't left him exhausted; instead, he was focused, organized, lean, efficient, committed, and in love with the property. The house, he was confident, would come along. In many ways he'd become a man I didn't recognize. I respected and admired him, but I didn't quite know him. Perhaps understandably, his personality seemed subsumed by his focus on the work facing him.

We weren't good partners to each other that month, and the cracks had shown through more than usual. On a rare night out in early December, after a disappointing meeting with the first kitchen planner, Noel and I went on a date to one of our favorite Indian restaurants. For some reason that night I was feeling more sorry for myself than usual. The pressures of putting together a kitchen for a house I didn't care about felt grossly unfair. On top of that was the pressure of a busy travel season at work. I had a bit of a pout. "I don't want to be doing this," I told him. "I resent the time."

Noel interrupted me, "We can't have this conversation. I don't have a choice here. We've made a decision. It's too late to wish we hadn't done it. We're doing it. I worry too, but I don't have the luxury of not plowing ahead. We don't have a choice anymore."

He was right, of course, and his quiet, truthful response put me to shame, but my feelings were real too. I understood theoretically why we couldn't have that conversation, but my frustration wasn't alleviated by the knowledge. Although I knew I was being childish, his brusqueness hurt. I fought tears through the entire meal, and Noel was furious with me as we left the restaurant. I didn't blame him. I wish I could say the project became clear to me after that night, that I made it my own. I wish I could say I never grumbled, or worried, or complained, or doubted again, but I can't. The country house was still not my vision of home, and I couldn't imagine it ever would be.

Home was still the pink house, where now as every year for almost a decade, we celebrated Christmas. Home was where I baked, as always, my Christmas breads and cookies, where I wrapped presents and took baskets to friends and neighbors. Unlike the Christmas fable in which the night before Christmas no one was stirring, not even a mouse, there was a mouse stirring. A little deer mouse had wandered into the country house that day. Noel had found him sitting on top of the tool table, nibbling on a cracker someone had left out. The mouse wasn't at all startled when he saw Noel; instead, he cocked his little head with what looked like curiosity and kept nibbling.

The pink house also entertained a stranger the night before Christmas, as for the first time Leif's fiancée joined us for our Christmas Eve celebration. Noel and I were resigned to their wedding in May, and I watched carefully that evening to see what my family would look like in the coming years. The prospect of being a mother-in-law was new to me. I'd given little thought to what an adjustment it might be to welcome a newcomer into the close circle of the family. I wanted to do so graciously, and I hoped I was succeeding despite all my misgivings.

T. had clearly given considerable thought to her gifts to all of us that night. It was evident that she'd studied us and our tastes and was making a heroic effort to become a part of the family. In light of her efforts, I was all the more chastened by my lingering doubts about the marriage.

As soon as Christmas was over, I headed to New Orleans for the annual Modern Language Association meeting, while Noel continued to work. Now, though, because of the labors of our good friends, the house was wired, the upstairs had some insulation, and Noel hoped to finish insulating before I returned home so he could finally run the furnace.

House on the Highway

DURING A BLIZZARD in early January shortly after my eleventh birthday, we moved away from Litchfield to a little rental house at the intersection of First Street and Omaha Avenue in Norfolk, Nebraska. Omaha Avenue was at that time the major truck route through town to Omaha, and First Street was a major north-south thoroughfare between downtown Norfolk and the industrial side of town. Our rental house was located only a few blocks from a slaughterhouse and a large stockyard. A mainline railroad track ran near the stockyards, close enough that the frequent trains rattled all the windows of our house day and night. On the street in front of the house, a seemingly never-ending parade of eighteen-wheelers screamed to a stop at the traffic light on the corner and, then, like fat men with emphysema, wheezed and coughed as they slowly gathered speed again to head out of town. The foundation of the house and all its walls vibrated with the weight of those trucks. There was no place to get away from the noise and the stench. My first response to the horror of this house the day we moved in was to hide as far as I could in the back of the closet in my parents' room.

Dad had decided to become a full-time minister and enrolled in a small Bible college in Norfolk to train Christian Church ministers. For the first time in my life I became conscious of money, or the lack of it. My father had to sell his remaining cattle when he'd gotten into financial trouble after the gas station had gone bust earlier that year.

The best thing about the house on the highway was a row of sapling trees growing close against the south windows of the kitchen. If I looked out those windows, I could pretend we were in the woods. No amount of imagination, though, could deny the reek of animals confined in too small a space in the stockyards, or the peculiar oppressive odor of animals being slaughtered and processed at the rendering plant, or the diesel fumes from the eighteen-wheelers on the highway only a few feet from our front door.

The house was much too small for us. In this one-story two-bedroom with no basement, my brothers slept on bunk beds in a tiny TV nook off the cramped living room. Dad hung a gray vinyl, sliding curtain for privacy. The bedroom my sister and I shared was the largest room in the house, large enough to hold my piano. I'd been playing the piano for six years by then, and I still played the alto saxophone. My requests for other lessons—dancing, gymnastics—would later be denied as too frivolous, but I knew even then that the real reason was a lack of money.

Shortly after the move, our parents took us with them to Sunset Plaza, the brand-new shopping mall in Norfolk. The mall was located more than two miles from our house. We'd never seen a shopping mall before. Fluorescent lights probed and illuminated every corner as though to prove there was no dirt anywhere. The waxed linoleum floors gleamed. My siblings and I slid on those slick floors until Dad told us to settle down. We quickly grew overheated in our winter coats but kept them on anyway as we followed our parents up and down aisles in store after store until I felt a new kind of fatigue. It wasn't the walking that tired me. I felt queasy and exhausted with excess. My siblings began to complain with the same frustration I was feeling. Except our parents weren't finished yet. They seemed energized by the plentiful shelves. And maybe that led to clouded judgment on their part, thinking that because the mall was enclosed it was safe. Maybe I'm only making excuses for what happened later, shifting the blame from myself. In any event, the four of us were left on a bench in the mall to wait as our parents continued to shop.

We waited and waited, watching the exits of the various stores for our parents to return. When, after what seemed like a long time, they still hadn't come for us, I panicked, and in my panic grew convinced Mom and Dad had forgotten us and left for home. As a few stores began to close, ringing down their metal doors and turning out their lights, I felt even more justified in my distorted reasoning.

At my insistence, we set out together that night in a strange city, in the freezing cold of the new year, to find our way home. We were completely unfamiliar with streetlights or street signs. I didn't (and still don't) have a good sense of direction; nor did I even know yet our new address. All I knew was the major intersection where we lived.

I have only a pale memory of our journey that night: dark streets, snowy sidewalks, empty parking lots, a few houses we passed in our long walk. I don't know how long it took or what we talked about on the way, if we talked at all. I only know we eventually arrived home. I had somehow guided all of us there as though by desperate instinct. When we reached the house, I was surprised to find the windows dark and the front door locked. As we waited together on the cold front stoop, I realized the gravity of my mistake.

Later, after a frantic search at the mall, following the advice of the security guards to check at home, our parents must have been shocked to discover the four of us there shivering with the cold on the front stoop. They were so relieved we were safe, they didn't punish me for my rash act. Or, perhaps it had been so unnerving, so preposterous, they couldn't think of a suitable response.

THE NEW SCHOOL we attended, Washington School, was a three-story brick building across the street from our house on the other side of First Street. Even at school we couldn't escape the oppressive sounds and smells of our life at home. Washington School was rough, and we were sheltered children.

The boys in my fifth-grade class were cruel in ways the boys in my small class at Litchfield hadn't been. A few of the boys who lived near the stockyards were the most threatening. In daily rounds through the playgrounds, they moved like a pack of hyenas, slugging designated girls hard with closed fists in the small aching plums of budding breasts and yelling, "Flatty," in an accusatory way. I was among those girls singled out for this abuse.

But I could run. I could run faster than anyone on the playground except Lisa Ronk. We raced in the dirt playground on the west side of the school under a row of shade trees next to the street. I never once beat Lisa Ronk, no matter how many races we ran in the next year and a half, but I was her only real contender.

Because of this, in the spring Dad challenged me to a race. "We'll see how fast you are," he said, making it clear he believed he could still outrun me. I always ran barefoot and took off my shoes and socks to stand beside him on the narrow sidewalk in front of our house waiting as my sister Tami yelled, "Get ready, get set, go." While semis roared by only a few feet away from us, we ran neck and neck toward the end of the block, wheezing and gasping along with the trucks, until my father fell. He fell suddenly and spectacularly. It took me awhile to realize what had happened before I slowed to a stop. He skinned his knee badly, a deep abrasion that would take months to heal. Afterward, Dad remained certain he would have beaten me had he not fallen.

The second half of my fifth-grade year and again in sixth grade, my teacher was a tall, awkward, redhead named Mrs. Horrocks. Because of overcrowding, our classroom both of those years was in an unused gym in the basement of the school. Mrs. Horrocks had learned I wrote plays and allowed me to stage them for the class. She allowed us extra time during class to design sets, and on those days when we performed my plays, my classmates pushed aside the wheeled chalkboards that divided the room to reveal the stage in the large space behind. The old gym housed an out-of-tune piano, and I sometimes accompanied what was happening onstage to create a desired dramatic effect.

THAT FIRST YEAR IN NORFOLK my parents seemed to disappear. Mom worked nights at Dale Electronics, a factory that made electronic resisters. She brought some of the resistors home to show us, tiny wire braids with colorful miniature beads on the ends. She told us about working with vats of acetate, a chemical so corrosive it would dissolve a Styrofoam cup in seconds. She knew. She'd tried it. In those months, she was tired and didn't seem like the same mother I'd known from before. Dad took classes in the mornings and worked from two to ten as a janitor at Norfolk Junior High School. He studied on weekends and when things were quiet at work. Our one reprieve was that for the first year we lived in Norfolk, Dad still preached every other Sunday in Litchfield, so twice a month we made the trip back home to Litchfield—rain or snow—to stay with my grandparents on the ranch. On those cold winter nights Grandma turned on the new electric blankets she'd bought for the beds in the unheated upstairs rooms.

I didn't question in those years why we were doing what we were doing. Nor did I ever hear my mother complain. She seemed to make the best of every situation, able to laugh at inconvenience as though it were nothing, rallying to the lost cause, encouraging Dad in his bouts of discouragement, his bursts of renewed hope, and the inevitable new enterprise.

Within six months after we moved into the house on the highway, Mom no longer worked on the floor of the factory but worked
instead as a secretary in the factory offices. She left the house those
mornings wearing a dress and nylons, her hair fixed. And by sixth
grade I was no longer afraid of the boys in my class at Washington
School. Instead, those tough Washington School boys now hung
out at our house after school, their bikes stacked beside mine on
our postage-stamp lawn.

The Bible college where my father was studying hosted many
events. I was enamored of the college's singing groups, especially
the Enthusiastics, a sort of swing choir fondly known as the Spas-
tics. One of the college's professors wrote musicals that the Spas-
tics performed. There were drums and electric guitars. Most of
the students at the college were trying to be hip without becoming
hippies. Hippies were dangerous. These college students were the
closest thing I'd seen to cool since Rhonda's older sister, Kathy. The
boys kept their hair one length in haircuts that just brushed their
collars, their thick bangs sweeping past their eyebrows flirting
with the college's dress code. The girls all had long, straight hair.
They wore heavy blue eye shadow and thick black lashes. Their
lips were painted pale pink or white. They wore dresses just above
the knee, a recent concession to style on the part of the school,
but there were strict admonitions and constant vigilance that their
dresses be no shorter. While around us the country raged with
student protests, the civil rights movement, the women's movement, upheavals in higher education, a world of change, I knew
only vaguely what was happening. It seemed to have nothing to
do with us.

In my sixth-grade year my father told me he'd met the perfect
man for me. He said it sarcastically when we were arguing one day.
In the new freshman class at the college was a student, Ross M.,
the oldest son of the college's longtime president. He was a smart

young man, known for being rebellious. Unlike others in that milieu, he was interested in what was happening in the wider world. He read outside of the narrow biblical canon and was as likely in a class discussion to quote Hegel or Heidegger as the book of Matthew. He read Salinger and Vonnegut, Beckett and Joyce. He was expelled his freshman year for drinking but returned the following year. I often saw him around town, his hair longer than the college's dress code allowed, always riding an English ten-speed, the first ten-speed I'd ever seen and one of the first in Norfolk. He climbed fourteen-thousand-foot mountains. He ran long distances, something few people did at that time. He was impossibly old at eighteen, and I had a terrible crush on him.

It appeared my father was right. Ross did seem to be the perfect man for me. Ross knew things I wanted to know, but I felt I was standing on the other side of a deep chasm from him. I couldn't imagine crossing that impossible rift, not so much to him as to what he knew, so I contented myself with watching him from afar.

January 2002

IN THE MONTHS SINCE 9/11 I'd been consumed, like many others, with thoughts of shelter, realizing yet again how important and fundamental shelter is to us. As 2002 began, I wanted to be hunkered down, to be careful with money, to make no sudden or bold moves; instead, I was regularly forced out of my comfort zone as we continued our work on the country house.

Noel is by no means a reckless or careless man. I had no reason not to trust him to see us through this undertaking, but I noted how this project had thrown into relief the real differences between us. Clearly neither of us would have or could have done this work alone. It was the marriage that had allowed it to happen. We were stronger together than we were apart. We had, over the years, brought out the best in each other. By most definitions, the marriage was good. But now, two months into this long project, I felt a subtle rift growing between us. Our differences had always seemed minor compared to our compatibility, but now we seemed marooned from one another, functioning still efficiently out of habit and discipline, but each of us adrift somehow from the other. I didn't always want to see that, though, and continued to believe we'd find our way back to each other once the dust, the literal dust in this case, had settled.

And I continued to fret over Leif's upcoming marriage. I felt as if I could read his future much as I might read a plot-driven novel.

The tragedy to come of that boy's life seemed clear; and, no stranger to the disaster caused by a wrongheaded marriage, I couldn't help but project my own past mistakes onto his decision. Leif has always been a dreamer: building, drawing, playing guitar, painting, writing. When he was in upper grade school, inspired no doubt by Tolkien, he began to draw intricately beautiful maps of fantasy worlds he created, complete with oceans, rivers, forests, and cities within states and countries. He developed complex languages and detailed social, political, and economic histories for each country. The languages were composed of lovely runes, and the maps he drew all bore not only the crests he'd designed of the important fictional families but the runes of those languages as well. We still found around the house, secreted in the woodwork and other strange hiding places, tiny scraps of paper with messages he'd written in these runes and hidden when he was a little boy.

It was inevitable that he would begin to write, and at thirteen he started a novel. Unfortunately, at that time we had only one computer. It had been my computer, and it was housed in a small upstairs room I claimed as my own. He began to write in the evenings, which had always been the time I'd set aside to write. And even if I could have negotiated that time, Leif colonized the office with the clutter of his projects, and I no longer felt it was the inviolable space it had once been.

This situation presented a terrible dilemma for me. At first there seemed only two alternatives, one worse than the other: sacrifice my work for his, a symbolic suicide; or tell him he couldn't use my space and risk his creativity for mine, a symbolic murder. Neither option seemed viable until I found the solution by accident. Unaware of my situation at home, a friend of mine one day mentioned his discipline of writing early each morning. I'm not a morning person, but in that instant I found the answer to my problem. I would *become* a morning person. For the next three years, until Noel renovated the basement and built a space for a second computer, I woke at 5:00 A.M. each morning to write.

NOW, IN JANUARY OF 2002, I believed that creative, gifted boy I'd tried so hard to protect was about to make a horrible decision. I felt strongly, despite her good qualities, T. would have little patience or sympathy for Leif's need to dream. The marriage, I suspected, would not be a shelter to him, or to her.

I was in this state of mind when Leif called me at the start of the year. "I have some news for you, Mom," he said. "I thought you should know, T. and I have postponed the wedding."

"Oh," I said, careful in my response.

He continued, his voice casual, "We're just too stressed out trying to get everything done by May. It's a lot more work than we realized."

"So what's the new date?"

"We don't have a new date. We've postponed it indefinitely."

"Okay," I said, catching my breath at the word "indefinitely." "Let me know when you set a date so I can get it on the calendar." Even as I spoke, I knew there'd be no wedding, and after hanging up the phone I immediately called Noel with the news. Like me, he interpreted the indefiniteness of the postponement as a sign the wedding wouldn't take place.

When I next saw T., she told a different story and talked about an autumn wedding. She seemed justifiably put out about Leif's equivocation. I understood her frustration. Leif had begun to make plans to travel with his friend for a month as soon as school was out in the spring. He was talking about getting an apartment with his sister Jordan that summer. All these arrangements not only excluded T. but also indicated he wasn't planning a life with her in the immediate future. To me, his behavior was only more

evidence of why he wasn't ready to get married. This was the pro-
verbial train wreck I'd feared all along, except suddenly there was
hope—for both of them. I sensed, for her sake as well as Leif's, T.
would come to see this for what it was and act accordingly. The one
thing I guessed, as cowardly as it sounded on Leif's part, was that
it would be T., not Leif, who would have to initiate the breakup.

WHILE THIS FAMILY drama unfolded, Noel's father returned to
help finish the framing and insulation. Shortly before Floyd arrived, Noel began to experience severe anxiety. He'd had normal
anxiety all along, understandably worried about money, time, and
his own ability to solve various problems on the project, but he'd
always been able to work in spite of it. Now, though, he was almost
crippled by anxious thoughts. He had difficulty sleeping, started
waking up in the middle of the night obsessively making lists and
rehearsing irrational fears, exhausted before his grueling days had
even started. Unlike the earlier anxiety, he couldn't seem to shrug
off his worries during the day.

Now it was my turn to be calm and confident. "Of course,
you can do this. Look at what you've done already. Look how far
you've come. You're on the downhill." As much as it was clear Noel
wanted to be encouraged, his anxiety only increased. I finally recommended he talk to our family doctor. Maybe she could prescribe
something to help, but Noel didn't want to be taking medication
and rejected that suggestion. We tried everything we could think
of, but in the end, it was only Floyd's calming presence, his ability to think through problems, and his knack for reassurance that
helped Noel turn the corner.

Floyd is a remarkable man and is widely considered a prince
among his friends and family members. In other words, those who
know him best and love him most—and none more so than Noel.

Floyd and his identical twin brother, Lloyd, were the youngest chil-dren in a large Mennonite family. He'd grown up on a farm near Milford, Nebraska, where Noel's cousin Leonard still lived. Noel's grandfather was a Mennonite minister and a farmer. Grandpa Eicher managed these responsibilities with an enormous physical handicap. He had only one leg. The missing leg had started out as a stunted limb, the result of childhood polio, but he'd so hated the uselessness of that ill-formed leg that as an adult he demanded it be amputated, a surgery performed on the kitchen table in the farmhouse, presumably without anesthesia.

These stories come down to us so regularly in the West it's hard to know what they mean exactly. All we know is that *if* there had been complaint or even perhaps adjustment made to com-pensate for that handicap, *if* Grandpa Eicher had been less stoic, the story might be told with shame instead of pride. A lot rides on that old man's lack of self-pity and weakness and that of all the other old-timers who were tough enough to make it in this inhospitable place. I suspect it was in part these attitudes that led Floyd to leave Nebraska at age eighteen and never return. As a fifth-generation Nebraskan, I too have inherited these stories. I have few models other than suffering stoically, and I must always question the role such attitudes play in putting up too long with bad situations.

The four sons in Floyd's family of origin all rebelled against their Mennonite roots. The older two dramatically and completely, while Floyd and Lloyd simply left the Mennonite tradition for other Protestant faiths. Floyd, though, has retained the gentle and peace-able traits valued in Mennonite theology and culture. He's always easy to have around, but I was never so grateful for his presence as I was during the early weeks of the new year of 2002.

For almost two weeks, Floyd stayed, working long days, going out to the house alone to finish insulating while Noel worked in town, and staying through the evening to help Noel finish the framing. Unaccustomed as he was to cold weather after living for more than twenty years in a warm climate, I suspect Floyd suffered those days, but he seemed to do so happily for Noel's sake. Or was it simply western stoicism?

THE BIGGEST FRUSTRATION for Noel during the framing had been the greenness of the two-by-fours he'd bought. Now, as he and Floyd finished insulating, many of those wet two-by-fours he'd framed with had begun to twist, and Noel regretted not having spent a bit more money to buy better quality boards. In addition, as he'd predicted in December, the framing was sometimes complicated because of the wiring; but with each evening's report about the progress of the work, he never failed to note how far behind he would have been had Bob and Cathy not done the wiring for him in December.

By the time Floyd left in mid-January, the house was completely insulated, and Noel gratefully turned on the furnace. Whatever anxieties had plagued him when the month began left with Floyd. The insulation was finished just in time, for we experienced more bad weather in late January, day after day of snow and freezing rain. Not only was Noel glad to be able to turn on the furnace, he was also glad for his four-wheel-drive Chevy, as each night he traveled on icy Highway 77 to and from the country house.

In the middle of the month, I again called Mr. Cox, the eccentric old man in Newman Grove and repeated the specifications for what we needed: six hundred square feet of four-inch fir flooring. "Do you have it?" I asked.

"I'm *pretty* sure," he said again.

"Could we come this Saturday to take a look?"

He paused. "Call me on Saturday morning. I'm not sure what

I'll be doing that day." I rolled my eyes as he spoke, but what could I do? I agreed to call him Saturday before leaving.

When I called Mr. Cox on Saturday morning, after a bit of hemming and hawing on his part, I finally pinned him down. He'd be home if we came at 2:00. That Saturday morning was unseasonably warm. The sun was shining, and already by 9:00 A.M. the temperature was sixty degrees. People were outside in shirtsleeves. At noon, as we prepared to leave Lincoln, Noel wanted to go without taking a coat, but I insisted he take one. In light of the unseasonable heat, he protested.

"It's January," I said. "We live in Nebraska. Remember the blizzard of 1888." It was all I needed to say. I'd been reminding my children since they were little in this way, too, that we live in a place where you can still die from the cold given the right circumstances.

As if to underscore the reasonableness of my admonition, within a half hour of leaving Lincoln, the wind suddenly grew fierce, bullying Noel's heavy truck so he had to fight to keep it on the road. The sky darkened, and the temperature plummeted. We regretted immediately not having grabbed, in addition to our coats, our winter hats, mittens, scarves, long johns, and warm socks. It didn't snow, but the temperature continued to drop. By the time we reached Newman Grove, the temperature was in the single digits, and the wind chill made it feel much colder.

That afternoon as we stood shivering on Mr. Cox's front porch, waiting for him to answer the door, he surprised us by coming around the back way instead. I knew it for what it was, an old trick of rural folks, checking out visitors without being seen. We apparently met the test, for he introduced himself. He was an elderly but still vigorous man, and he told us the flooring was in a former hog barn on his son's place about a mile down the road. He explained how all the buildings on his farmstead were full of salvage materials, and he was now filling the buildings on his son's farm as well. "I've got four buildings in town, too, if you'd like to see them later. You mentioned something about wanting old interior doors. I've got those in town. I've got lots of doors."

The old hog barn was a long narrow building with a low ceiling and a haymow accessed from outside by a ladder; he'd stored flooring on both levels. Mr. Cox, having noted our unpreparedness both for the cold and for handling the wood, found two pairs of extra work gloves in his truck. "You'll need these," he said as he handed them to us.

The flooring was in excellent condition. I could tell without his saying anything Noel was pleased with it. Once we'd culled through the short pieces stored on the main floor, Mr. Cox climbed the flimsy wood ladder into the haymow and from there handed down to Noel long boards two at a time. Noel carefully looked over each one before handing it to me to stack in the truck, sorted by length. Occasionally he handed one of the boards back up to Mr. Cox as unacceptable.

The truck was full by the time we'd loaded all we needed. The flooring was expensive, but we were thrilled to have it, confident it would sand out well and certain it would match the existing floors in the house.

Despite being miserable with the cold, we consented to follow Mr. Cox into Newman Grove to look at his other buildings. He took us through the first two buildings, both unheated. The enormous spaces were filled with every salvage item imaginable: hardware for any conceivable use, light fixtures, cupboards, balusters, banisters, tubs and sinks, medicine chests, door plates, porch columns, gingerbread for exteriors, windows, interior and exterior doors, all sorts of trim board for inside and out, more flooring. Although things were kind of sorted by type, the true logic of the place was a mystery, and the only key Mr. Cox himself. He took us right to anything we mentioned.

As he'd promised, he'd accumulated a lot of interior doors, and if we'd been suffering less from the cold, we might have enjoyed looking thoroughly. But we saw nothing that inspired us, and we knew there were no deals here, only the hard-to-find item we were willing to pay dearly to have.

At this point in the project, we were still discussing the aesthetics of the house. The kitchen had ended up being very contemporary. If we'd had more time to salvage, I might have tried to find old cupboards and attempted to restore the kitchen more, but given the constraints of time, it hadn't made sense.

I was still considering the possibility of hanging old interior doors and preserving their unique patinas as a way to make the house feel more like an old farmhouse. While Noel appreciated what I was hoping to do, he hadn't been enthusiastic about the idea. Not only did he not believe we could find enough interior doors the right size in the time we had, he also dreaded the tinkering required to hang all those doors and make the hardware work. I'd known from the beginning the odds were against this concept, but until being at Mr. Cox's and seeing more vintage interior doors than I'd ever seen before, few of which seemed a remote possibility, I hadn't had to admit it. Now I knew it wasn't going to happen. The question of doors would continue for many weeks with new questions: Painted or stained? Six panel? Four panel? Three panel? What sort of hardware?

We drove home that evening, the back of the truck piled high, gratified to have found flooring and pleased to have encountered a character like Mr. Cox. He knew the worth of the items he'd salvaged, and he knew how to store things properly so as to avoid damage. It was no surprise to us that restoration carpenters from both Lincoln and Omaha regularly sought him out as they began work on new projects.

FOR WEEKS, LARRY, the Psychos' lead guitarist, had been asking if there was anything he could do to help Noel. Larry is a meticulous man, skilled at the most delicate of tasks. Noel and I have often felt that if he weren't an English professor, he'd have been a great luthier—repairing stringed instruments. He seems to have endless patience for the kind of precision work that drives Noel mad. When he volunteered to help lay the replacement flooring throughout the house, Noel knew it was a job perfectly suited to Larry's temperament. That first day, just as he and Larry had started the project, Noel was called into work to load a train. This was only the beginning. By the end of the month of January, there would be eight trains to load, most of them requiring Noel to work late into the night or on his precious weekends. In this situation, though, Larry was fine to continue alone. He kept at the fastidious work, tearing out damaged wood and laying replacement boards so no one would ever notice they hadn't been part of the original floor. Later, he admitted to Noel he had loved working alone in the quiet of the country place.

Once the damaged floorboards in the house had been replaced and before Noel tore out the kitchen floor, Tracy from the grain elevator returned to help reframe the kitchen so it would be square for the new cabinets. After years of working together, Tracy and Noel could solve almost any problem with few words.

THROUGH THE PAST FEW months while working on the house, Noel had become acquainted with our new neighbors, Mark and Linda. Now and then Mark wandered up to check on Noel's progress, while Linda occasionally brought him a plate of food. Weeks earlier, in November, Mark, a plumber by trade, had told Noel he wanted to plumb the house for us. Now in late January, after having quietly monitored Noel's progress with the framing, Mark arrived one Saturday morning with his tools and began to rough in the plumbing.

"He's an artist," Noel told me with admiration that night. "You have to see how he's run the copper pipes. Everything's perfectly symmetrical, perfect forty-five degree angles." Noel shook his head. As he told me about Mark's work, just as when he described Larry's equally skilled, careful work on the flooring, Tracy's patience and ingenuity with problem solving, Bob and Cathy's work wiring, and his father's help and good cheer, he choked up a little. I understood his emotion without his saying anything more. "It's like an old-fashioned barn raising," I said. He nodded, then slowly shook his head. "I'll never be able to repay all of this." But as a friend had said when she'd heard about the generosity of our friends and neighbors, "Noel has good handyman karma." And it was true. Through the years, Noel had helped many people with projects that were simple to him but overwhelming for them, and I knew in the years to come he'd be there again to help as needed. For now, though, it humbled both of us to have received so much.

At the end of the month we heard that the pink house had been selected for the Near South Neighborhood Association President's Award. The Association annually recognizes a house in the Near South that exemplifies the neighborhood's goal of renovation and restoration. Perhaps it was a not-so-subtle sign of my own shifting energies when instead of becoming nostalgic, I simply said in response to news of the award, "Maybe this will help us when it comes time to sell."

The French surrealist poet Robert Desnos believed it was important to look for the marvelous in everyday life. He also believed in the need to "premeditate our happiness." These ideas are meaningful to me. The marvelous is everywhere. I saw it in many ways at this time. When I told a friend that Leif and his fiancé had indefinitely postponed their wedding, her eyes widened in amazement.

"I think you may be a bit of a witch," she said. While she was grant-
ing me too much power, I understood what she meant. I'd wanted
something very much—to protect my son—and it seemed my wish
had been granted. But there were other marvels, too: snow-covered
fields stark against the blue winter sky; a dead tree that looked like
a woman standing in a canoe; a man on a Lincoln street walking
simultaneously a Rottweiler and a Chihuahua of the same color.

I'm better at celebrating the marvelous in everyday life than I
am at premeditating happiness, though. Most of the time I can
honestly say I'm happy, but hard experience has left me with a
strong urge to predict the worst. I have a profound need not be
caught off guard. In the past few months, I'd taken as careful stock
as I could for our future. I felt I knew what the worst things could
be. None of them were life threatening, though some of them were
financially ruinous. In the wake of 9/11, like many around me, I'd
taken stock of the country's future, too, and, given my temperament, I was aware of a growing dis-ease when George Bush, in his
state of the union address at the end of this month, delivered his
dire warnings about the "axis of evil." To anyone listening, he was
preparing us for war. I wondered how as a country we had come to
this point, how we could possibly hope to fight all the potential ills
of the world, how in fact we could fight an emotion—terror—and
how this new trend toward preemption could make us safer. I felt
not only my own shudder that night at his words but also a shudder across the world.

House on Logan Street
NORFOLK, NEBRASKA, 1971–1973

THE SUMMER BEFORE I started junior high, I woke one night in my bunk in the girl's dorm at Pibel Bible Camp and in the darkness saw all the beds in the dorm were empty except mine. Terrified, I climbed down from my bunk and walked up the middle aisle and back again just to be sure. No one. I was alone in the middle of the night. I tried to console myself. Maybe everyone was meeting in the chapel. Maybe they'd tried to wake me and couldn't. Still in my nightgown, I ran out the screen door, down the sandy path to the chapel only to find it dark and empty. I ran to the showers, to the outdoor privies, to the cafeteria. Around me the only sound I heard was the booming of the bullfrogs on the lake. Maybe there was a baptism. Maybe someone in the middle of the night had felt an urgent need for salvation. I ran to the beach at the lake where baptisms took place. No one. Only the cold stars and the water lapping against the shore. Or maybe, I thought for a moment with horror, everyone else had been taken up in the Rapture, and I had been left behind.

One final desperate thought. The nurse. I ran to her cabin and knocked on the screen door. What sweet relief when I heard her sleepy voice say, "What is it?"

"There's no one in the dorm," I said through the screen. I watched as she got out of bed and wrapped a robe around her nightgown. "I'm all alone," I said after she unhooked the latch of the screen door.

She looked at me closely for a second. "Honey," she said, "You're just dreaming." She gently steered me back toward the girl's dorm. "See," she said once we reached the door. "They're all here."

I looked through the screen and saw she was right. "They're here after all," I said.

She nodded. "Go back to bed now."

I walked quietly back to my bunk, my cold, sandy feet and my sopping nightgown evidence I'd actually gone to all the places I'd seen in my dream. My first and last episode of sleepwalking.

That same summer my family moved away from the cramped house on the highway to a quiet house on Logan Avenue. My sister and I each had our own basement bedrooms. We all found it funny that, like the house on the gravel road, we once again lived across the street from a high school football field. On autumn evenings the amplified voice of the announcer echoed across our roof in waves. A large practice field separated us from the noise of the crowd itself.

I was restless that entire summer, waiting for something. I didn't know I was looking for a friend until I saw her across the room after band practice, the first day of junior high. I'd noticed her immediately in the third row of the clarinet section. She was very petite, so tiny in fact that she wore as a dress a yellow poor-boy shirt belted with a gold chain. Her blonde hair was bobbed just beneath the ears. I'd always found the clarinet a silly instrument, and she played hers with a comical earnestness. I couldn't account for the fierce determination I felt to meet her, but I didn't question it.

After rehearsal, despite my rush to get to the next class period, I pushed through other students disassembling their instruments in the band storeroom, my alto saxophone still dangling by its neck strap. I finally found her in the corner taking apart her clarinet. The same earnestness I'd seen earlier was also evident in that task. With courage unusual for me, I introduced myself. I thought she was the most magical girl I'd ever seen. She looked up at me, slightly distracted, not particularly thrilled at the interruption and clearly not as enthralled with me as I was with her. "I'm Joy," she said and snapped her case shut. "See you."

When I discovered later that week we were also in the same gym class, I experienced again the same happiness I'd felt the first time I'd seen her in the band room. She hadn't yet bought her gym suit and was wearing her street clothes—a navy skirt, a white blouse with blue and gold epaulettes on the shoulders, nylons, and navy flats—while I and the other girls wore the regulation red jumpsuits. My mother had found mine secondhand. In addition to being several sizes too big for my skinny frame, the legs ended in elastic so they resembled bloomers rather than shorts. I knew I looked ridiculous.

My determination conquered self-consciousness, and when we were given extra time at the end of the class, I immediately ran to greet Joy. She didn't remember me, and I had to reintroduce myself. Undeterred, I asked what grade school she'd attended. That's when I learned she'd just moved to Norfolk. Her parents were divorcing, and she'd moved with her mother and two sisters from Millard. She was homesick. They'd left their big house to live in a small two-bedroom her grandmother owned. Her father was a minister, she told me. There'd been terrible fights before her mother left.

"My father's a minister too," I said.

"What church?"

"Christian."

"Disciples? Non-Instrumental?"

The fact that she knew to make these distinctions already meant she knew more about the denomination than most people did. "Independent," I said, and her eyes lit up.

"That's my church, too." We chattered nonstop for the remainder of the class, at one point in our glee clasping hands and skipping around the gym, fast friends from that moment forward.

THAT YEAR, I ABRUPTLY stopped writing. I kept doing everything else I'd previously enjoyed, but suddenly writing seemed to me not only silly but somehow offensive. I wrote only if required to for an assignment or a test and then begrudgingly. I still played the piano and sang. I played saxophone in the concert and jazz bands. That year I had the lead role in the school's one-act play, and I served on the yearbook staff. At the time my writing silence seemed entirely natural. I didn't question it; nor did I feel saddened by it. I didn't see it as a loss but instead something I'd outgrown like my Sting-Ray bike.

Besides, I was busier than I'd ever been. When I wasn't doing school activities and spending time with friends, I was babysitting and working as a carhop at Louie's Tastee Treat. Joy and I met every Saturday morning on foot or on bicycle at a point midway between our houses. Our ritual on those Saturdays had evolved over many months, and we rarely altered it. We stopped first at the day-old-bread store, where we bought a twin pack of pecan pies, one for each of us. Then we went to the mall, the same mall where only two years earlier, I'd believed my parents had ditched my siblings and me. We foraged through the sale bins at Woolworth's finding small treasures each week: false eyelashes, wax mustaches, small bottles of perfume. We sometimes had our pictures taken together in the instant processing booth.

Once we'd exhausted our time at the mall, we walked to a nearby nursing home, where we'd adopted several elderly residents: Pierre, Maude, John, Elma, and June.

Later, on our way home, we stopped at Jax diner, where we

always shared a bowl of ham and navy bean soup. Neither of us much liked this soup, but somehow it resonated with our parent's stories of having grown up during the Depression.

We went to movies with our group of friends: *Tales from the Crypt, The Panic in Needle Park, Love Story.* We all read *Jonathan Livingston Seagull,* who became our hero; and when later most of us worked together as carhops at Louie's Tastee Treat, we developed a high-pitched seagull screech that accompanied simulated flight, our arms flapping, as we walked across the parking lot to take orders from customers. We were oblivious to how this behavior must have appeared to others, and Louie didn't put a stop to it.

Dad was still a student at the Bible college. The year I turned thirteen he began a student ministry in Clearwater, a small town fifty miles west of Norfolk in the northern Sandhills. Our family usually drove up only on Sunday mornings and spent the day there through evening services. My parents, ever conscious of having four children and not wanting to be a burden to church members, had moved a camper trailer onto the farm of a couple who were members of the church. There we cooked our own meals and occasionally stayed over on a Saturday night if necessary.

The farm where we parked the camper was owned by Donald and Lila Johring. Donald and Lila raised sheep and cattle. Donald looked as though he might have been just as comfortable in the outback of Australia as he was in the northern Sandhills of Nebraska. He was tall, tanned, and rugged, with an aquiline nose and ice-blue eyes. Lila looked like a throwback to the 1930s with her old-fashioned dresses, outdated finger-wave hairstyle, and rimless glasses. She taught in a one-room school (one of the few remaining in the state) just down the road from their house and was the church's Sunday school superintendent. She constantly rushed around appearing not to discriminate between what had to be done and what could be left undone: vacuuming out empty boxes, washing out used plastic bags of every sort, keeping and reusing everything, fussing all the while as though everyone's well-being depended on these economies.

Being in Clearwater was like stopping time in many ways. It was as though the 1970s was another galaxy. At Clearwater Church of Christ I was not only sullen, I was at my most argumentative. The Sunday school teacher was a simple woman, whose baby-talk voice drove me crazy. My sour attitude confused her. We didn't have a youth group, but when for a time a young man with a shock of blonde hair and thick black glasses took on the role of teaching the youth at night, I made no secret of my loathing for him. "He's an idiot," I told my parents and did nothing to hide my contempt.

I raged in the car those Sunday evenings as we drove home to Norfolk. Oddly, my parents indulged this venting, some of it anyway. "Let me stay in Norfolk for church," I begged, but on this Dad was firm. "You're the minister's daughter. It wouldn't look right. You need to attend church with the family."

I wanted to go to church in Norfolk, where Joy and my other friends were in a Sunday school class together and on Sunday evenings attended youth group, where the other kids weren't all strange the way they were at Clearwater. They did fun things together like bowling, roller skating, swimming, sledding. Their youth minister was funny, and students from the college served as interns. Ross M., the son of the Bible college president, now about to graduate, was everyone's favorite intern. Like me, all my friends had crushes on him.

Only Joy, it seemed, understood how I felt about Clearwater. She'd seen for herself the silly congregation, the ugly church building, the ridiculous singing. If we weren't careful, we'd get the giggles during church service there. Anything could set it off— Babe Jones's high notes careening off key, the elders and deacons shuffling toward the front of the church, their suits ill-fitting, their shoes dusty, their hair brushed flat, their foreheads white from wearing caps during the week. The women scurried about preparing tables for potlucks, planning endless, ridiculous programs.

The congregation at Clearwater confused me, though. While I loathed it, I also often felt a kind of sympathy for them. There was something simple and innocent about many of those adults, and I felt my own scorn like that of the mean kids on the playground making fun of other kids.

IT WAS AROUND this time I heard the full details of the story of Armageddon from Joy's stepfather. A southerner with a southerner's sense of drama and elaboration, he told us about the book of Revelation. Without equivocation, this *was* going to happen, every bit of it, just the way St. John had seen it in his vision on the Island of Patmos. The graves would open, the dead would rise. A hellish cast of characters would cause the world endless suffering: the dragon, the beast, the anti-Christ.

At thirteen, I was primarily concerned with the suffering he described and didn't take much note of the promises for eternal peace and bliss that would follow the years of tribulation. With an adolescent's preoccupation with the grotesque, I became fascinated. I was drawn to the details of the prophesied end of time in much the way I was drawn to horror movies. The delicious sensation of being scared out of my wits fit perfectly with the intensity of emotion I was experiencing in other areas of my life in those years.

Together with my friends from the church in Norfolk, I obsessed about the spectacular end we imagined. We recounted the gruesome details. It wasn't only us, though, for the early 1970s marked an increased fascination with predictions of the apocalypse. Of the many books by conservative believers, each one was more graphic than the next. I read them all, and I loved them. I was waiting for the inevitable end, hoping, as the premillenialists prophesied, that believers would be taken up—Raptured—before the seven years of tribulation began. But just in case I had to suffer through the tribulation, I read Richard Wurmbrand's *Tortured for Christ*, a graphic account of his ordeal behind bars in the communist bloc, and *The Dawn Must Come*, the story of a female missionary doctor's ordeal in the Congo when she was raped and driven from her camp. I was riveted by these accounts of faith and endurance in light of the quickly approaching end of time, and I became consumed with religious fervor, set to become a martyr for Christ.

Around that time, I had a dream about the Rapture. I dreamt I was walking on the streets of a large city, no city I recognized. It was a gray day, very dreary, when suddenly the wind began to whip about among the crowds of people. Above us the sky suddenly filled with black helicopters. The sound was deafening. Without warning, I felt myself pulled hard—as if by magnetic force—to my knees. I saw that everyone else around me had also been pulled to their knees. We covered our ears against the noise of the helicopters. In the dream, I exchanged a glance with a woman beside me on the sidewalk. "I wonder if this is the Rapture," I said. The woman only nodded. The feeling during this dream and for weeks afterward was one of terror and euphoria, for I had known without a doubt, as I shivered and cowered there on the sidewalk, that I would be allowed to board one of those black helicopters and would be spared all sorts of horrors—literally, saved by my faith.

TWO YEARS LATER, my family would move again. I was fifteen and just starting high school when Dad accepted a position as the full-time pastor for a new church in Kearney. It would be his first and his last job as a full-time minister. The young congregation that had called him was divisive from the beginning. The work became both dispiriting and stressful. A couple of years after I graduated from high school, his health deteriorated. Diagnosed with congestive heart failure, he was forced to resign.

But here is where I lose myself. Here is where I seem to fall down the rabbit hole. For reasons I still can't quite grasp, things went terribly wrong. Even as I felt out of step during those years, a stranger in a strange town, it must not have seemed like that to those looking on from the outside. Outwardly, I was the model of high school success. I did all the things girls my age were supposed to do. By my senior year, I was the secretary of the choir, the president of the band, first chair alto saxophone in concert and jazz bands, a member of an elite drill team, homecoming queen, wrestling sweetheart, the girlfriend of a popular athlete. But inwardly, I had lost something vital in the move from Norfolk. I never recovered a close band of friends like those I'd had in Norfolk. I became overidentified with my father's failing ministry. I felt oddly resigned. I was desperately sad but had no way of articulating or even knowing what was wrong.

When at the end of my senior year I was offered a four-year scholarship to Kearney State College, I turned it down to attend instead the same unaccredited Bible college my father had attended. Although I had no interest in attending this college and had by this time come to have a low regard for it, I felt a strange and wrongheaded sense of duty to the kids in my youth group, new converts all, who had been persuaded to attend this college because of the church. When many of my high school teachers, dismayed by my choice, tried to reason with me, I refused to hear their arguments. I remember the summer after high school graduation feeling my own resignation, my depression, like a weight across my shoulders. It seemed I'd become at last, as I'd so fervently hoped only a few years before, a martyr for Christ.

February 2002

FEBRUARY IN NEBRASKA defines the dregs of winter. The world is cold and ugly, and everyone has lost hope for any possibility of spring. The streets and sidewalks, if they're not covered with snow and ice, are stained by the residue of the salt used liberally after snowstorms.

Even on the coldest days I walked to work. Like all people familiar with the cold, I'm adept at layering. My long-ago experience mountain climbing with my ex-husband taught me to regulate body heat with a hat. Hat-hair was inevitable for me in the winter. A few years ago, when my friend Theresa took a trip to India, she brought me back a fabulous cashmere shawl, and I'd discovered that this shawl, when used to cover both my nose and my mouth, made me almost impervious to the cold. I always wore two layers of socks inside my Canadian fur boots.

As might be clear from this description of my dress, I found, and still find, walking in winter a great privilege. I love being bundled against the cold, all the better if there has been snow. I like the muffled sounds and the feeling of being alone in the world, since, on especially cold days in a city like Lincoln where everyone drives, few other pedestrians venture out in the residential areas. As I walked that February, my thoughts were divided between my usual late winter weariness with the cold and an acute awareness that my days of walking to work were coming to an end.

By the start of the month the framing and insulating were finished at the country house. Drywall was next. We were almost halfway through the time allotted us on the bridge loan, but as we took stock of our progress, it seemed certain we weren't halfway through the work. No matter how we inventoried what we'd done and what remained to be done, we felt we were behind schedule.

Noel's worst day on the project had to have been a Saturday early in February. The kind intentions of people resulted in too much help. I could see that a familiar loss of control threatened to overwhelm him that day as four crews of two descended on the project to help with dry walling: my two brothers, Cam and Tad; Tracy and Rick from the elevator; Bob Blomstrom and Leif; and Noel and me. Throw in my mother bringing lunch for everyone and our neighbor Mark plumbing in the shower of the little bathroom, and suddenly the house was very crowded.

Under the best circumstances dry walling is stressful, heavy work. (Noel and I like to joke that we rehearse for hanging Sheetrock by taking a piece of the heavy drywall into the yard and swearing.) Cam and Tad were having a good time that day teasing and jostling each other, but even they settled down once they noticed how stressed Noel was. Inexplicably, all four teams had decided to start hanging Sheetrock in the kitchen at the same time. Nine people, including Mark, all crowding into one room with huge sheets of drywall, quickly equaled chaos. We shuffled and struggled and were otherwise ridiculous, and the fact that we were sharing two screw guns among the four teams only partially explained our behavior. No one seemed to be listening to anyone else, and it was clear that Noel was hesitant to tell volunteers what to do.

When I clumsily broke off the fragile end of a piece of drywall that Noel had painstakingly cut to fit into the corner around the washer and dryer, he lost it. Noel isn't a patient man under any circumstances, and although he often diffuses tension with humor,

he couldn't seem to do so that day. This sort of haphazard non-
sense didn't sit well with him, and I could tell he was conflicted
between his feelings of gratitude and his frustration about how
things were being done. I imagine there are times when Noel
wishes he were different, but he isn't someone who can pretend to
feel what he doesn't.

The craziness didn't last long. Eventually my brother Cam, a
serious bird-watcher who teaches science, went for a walk around
the property with Mom. Leif left for work. Rick left for another
obligation. Shortly after the episode of my breaking the drywall, I
decided I was in the way and dropped out. That left Bob and Tad
and Noel and Tracy to work together, two efficient and experienced
teams. Despite the rough beginning, by the end of the day they'd
made significant headway with a heavy, difficult job.

Over the next few days, I assisted Noel in finishing some of
the dry walling on the main floor: both bathrooms, the entryway,
and the hallway, as well as the ceilings. We'd dry walled ceilings
alone in the pink house, and I wasn't looking forward to the job.
In the past, we'd used the simple method of a T-bar and ladder, but
for this job, we wisely decided to rent a drywall hoist. It made all
the difference. Bob, Tracy, and Floyd—who returned again in mid-
February—helped finish the difficult work of Sheetrocking the upstairs. With its knee walls and pitched ceiling, it required careful
measurements and many cuts.

Throughout the month, in whatever spare time we could afford,
we continued to search for flooring for the concrete slab in the addition. Noel was concerned that without a crawl space beneath it,
the slab could sweat and cause damage to some kinds of flooring.
We looked seriously at cork tiles and at wool carpeting before con-
cluding ceramic tile was the best choice. We looked and looked,
changed our minds time and again, until finally Noel came home
from a trip to Omaha with a tile we thought resembled lightly

stained concrete. It was simple yet interesting. We laid out the four sample pieces in various places throughout the pink house. It looked good under our area rugs, and it looked all right against the primitive piece we'd decided on for the sink cabinet in the little bathroom. We bought it. Six hundred twenty-five square feet of tile to go in the addition, in the new entryway, and in the little bathroom off the kitchen. Tracy, from the elevator, took his truck to Omaha to help Noel transport the tile to the country house since that amount of tile weighed too much for one truck to haul.

Of all Noel's perfectionism, he's perhaps most particular about taping and mudding Sheetrock and in a strange way had been looking forward to this part of the project since we'd started. I think he saw it as a comfort, doing a mindless, routine task—much needed mental relief from other aspects of the project in which he'd felt barely one step ahead of where he needed to be. Knowing this about Noel, when Bob Blomstrom offered to help with the taping and mudding, he insisted he'd leave the last coat of mud for Noel, adding, "I know what a perfectionist you are." Noel didn't have the heart to tell him the first coat of mud was the most important in his technique and placing the tape properly from the beginning was what made all the difference in the last coat.

It must have been a miserable job for Bob to tape all the seams of the knee joints in the upstairs; and, in Noel's mind, Bob's method seemed not only to take more time but also to make a bigger mess than the method Noel had perfected over many years of repairing old plaster walls in the pink house. There were evenings after Bob left for the night when I walked with Noel through the upstairs wondering how the seams would ever become smooth with Bob's practice of applying a lot of mud (with which he mixed a bit of plaster of Paris) and then doing a lot of sanding—the opposite of Noel's method, which required as little mud as possible and consequently little sanding. Bob surely sensed Noel was not completely comfortable with his work and ended up taping and sanding only the upstairs. Of course, once Bob had finished, the walls looked great. His approach had simply thrown Noel off. When he started, Noel estimated he could finish the mudding in three weeks; but once I applied our formula, I guessed that, like everything else, it would take him twice as long. As the month unfolded, it became obvious he'd be lucky to finish even in six weeks.

I felt as though I hardly saw Noel anymore. For four and a half months he'd been at the country house every evening until late and every weekend, too. I'd understood from the beginning this was how it would be, but still I missed him. Months of hard work had made him even more fit and muscular. When I was working with him sometimes, I stole glances at him the way I might have a boy I had a crush on in junior high school. I was a little in awe of him. I've always had a weakness for people absorbed in their work, people who approach problems with gravity and have mastery of skills I don't possess. Noel's intensity, his seriousness, made my heart melt. I was more in love with him than ever. Sometimes it felt like a silly weakness, my willingness to love again with such abandon, but it was a wonder in a way, too. My heart had been scarred, and Noel had brought comfort and relief after years of hurt. I could never take that lightly.

While we worked, we listened to the radio. National Public Radio was fine for news and some talk programs, but we tired of the classical music favored by the Lincoln station. We listened to KZUM, the community radio station, and to college radio, and, strangely, we began to listen to country radio. I'd always despised country music, and Noel, old punk rocker that he is, had too. But somehow during certain phases of the project only country music seemed right. The sentimental, simplistic songs sometimes suited my mood, but not all the time. There were occasions when one or the other of us groaned with embarrassment over a song and, suddenly fed up with the overprocessed studio sound, begged the other to "turn that stupid dial."

One song in particular got on my nerves that winter, Toby Keith's song of vengeance after 9/11. It invoked every national icon in violent retribution for the terrorist attacks and was in sync with the vengeful, nationalistic mood afoot in the country. At the time, Noel argued that Keith was being ironic. "It's how we are," he said, as though I hadn't noticed. I thought he was giving Keith more credit than he deserved. The song was popular, and it never failed to make me furious.

I had thought Noel was a country boy the first time I saw him. I remember thinking he seemed out of place that summer night in July when he came into the foreign film theater at the university. During the five years I'd been a volunteer at the theater I had never talked to a patron I didn't know. Except once.

Noel was hard to miss that evening. Despite the heat, he was wearing a seed-corn cap, a long-sleeved shirt, and jeans. He looked like a farm boy. Because of my rural background, I should know better than most people there's no such thing as a typical farmer. Still, it was peculiar that someone so young would be *dressed* in his farm clothes to go out for the evening

He got my attention, I'll admit that. He was tall (six feet three inches) and handsome. I said something to him that I suppose, looking back, he interpreted as a line. I hadn't meant it to be. He lingered a bit by the door to talk to me, and I wasn't sure what to make of him. Still, because of this encounter, when I sat down in the back row before the movie started, I looked for where he was sitting in the theater. The lights hadn't gone down yet, and I watched as he removed his seed-corn cap and a mop of curly dark hair fell to his shoulders. He put on a pair of wire-rimmed glasses, and suddenly he was transformed. Already I'd begun to suspect he wasn't quite what he seemed.

We ended up walking together on campus that night after the film. I was so engrossed in our conversation I spent most of the evening walking with my head down in concentration, and afterward what I remembered best about him were his boots and his voice. I learned in our conversation he was working only temporarily on his family's ancestral farm in Nebraska. He still had an apartment in San Francisco, where he'd lived for a decade. It was clear he was looking for a change but didn't quite know what he wanted. His dream of being a farmer had been based on a fantasy, and those dreams had quickly evaporated once he learned the economic realities of farming. He derisively called himself that night a "wannabe farmer." He thought it was a little pretentious. I'd never known anyone who thought the wish to be a farmer was pretentious. He was a peculiar one, and I knew I'd met a singular human being.

Among the many things we discussed as we walked together that night was our mutual experience of growing up in fundamentalist Christian homes. Both of us felt we'd been damaged in some way by it. As we separated that evening, we made no plans, and I thought, without particular regret, I'd never see him again. Life is full of such encounters, and they don't always come to anything. I simply treasured meeting someone I felt was remarkable.

When he called me a month later, I was surprised and at the same time felt it was completely natural. In the weeks and months after that, the relationship grew in ways unique in my history of relationships. We'd met at a low point in both our lives. Neither of us would have been considered a catch by most of the world's standards. He was adrift, and I was still mired in the custody battle that would dominate our life together for the next year. Noel accepted me where I was at the time. He was supportive and encouraging, and I felt both liberated and sheltered in his love.

The differences between us were clear immediately, though. His father had worked for the airlines, and he'd spent every summer of his childhood traveling widely. He modestly explained it was less expensive for them to go to Europe on their free passes than to travel in the states by car. His mother was a professor and valued higher education. His childhood in Colorado had been full of adventure: mountain climbing, camping, swimming in lakes and rivers, skiing every weekend in the winter. He'd gone away to boarding school for his high school years. In his twenties, he continued a life of adventure, traveling the world, living in Los Angeles and northern California before finally graduating from San Francisco State, working and going to clubs in San Francisco, simply enjoying being young and single in an exciting city.

My twenties had been spent raising children and plugging away on my degrees: first my BA, then an MA (and eventually a PhD). I'd patiently plugged away for years to realize my dreams. Noel, however, was of a different stripe. He hadn't necessarily been ambitious in establishing goals of the sort I'd come to respect. He valued experience more than knowledge and action above contemplation, which didn't mean he wasn't thoughtful. To the contrary. I recognized immediately his quick intelligence, his sharp, sly wit, his fearless trust in his own observations, and his keen discernment about people and what they produce.

The eventual renovation of the pink house and now the rebuilding of the country house were the most dramatic, overarching goals Noel had established for himself. He'd thrown himself into both projects with intense focus, abandoning himself completely to the work. As a mother, I'd always had to temper my ambitions, always aware of the risks of neglecting my children, fighting for my goals only in the margins of my life, keeping them almost private from the family, and unwilling that others should have to sacrifice for my desires. I went too far with that, I'm sure, but only by fragmenting my life in those ways had I felt I could accomplish what I wanted to.

In my feeble attempts to describe it to myself in the first days of our relationship, I decided it felt geometric, as though we were opening up to each other and into new spaces. I'm still not able to describe it, but I knew that we were building something together even then and that, although the relationship felt precious, a little fragile at times, beneath it I sensed a strong foundation. It felt as though we were building a space in which our relationship could flourish.

So now in this February as we built together an actual house, I saw it as an extension of our love for one another, an expression of our solidarity in the world.

House at the Hundredth Meridian
COZAD, NEBRASKA, JANUARY 23, 1978

THE SUMMER AFTER my first and only year of Bible college, I took a job washing dishes in a nursing home. That's how I encountered Leroy, a deaf resident no one had spoken to for the ten years he'd lived there. A few times a year, his niece came to visit, but she could only finger spell, so their conversations were limited to smiles and nods, as they sifted through family photographs, pointing and spelling laboriously.

I first saw Leroy in the dining hall. He was sitting by himself at a table distant from the others. His manner, though, was not aloof; he watched the other tables with interest, his blue eyes bright and aware. I made an excuse to take something to him one day. It might have been tapioca in a beige Melmac bowl or lemon cake on a green Melmac plate. I set it down and signed to him. First the expression of shock, someone breaking the silence after so many hermetic years, then the smile, hands flying, a gush to communicate after unimaginable silence.

I attribute my promotion at the nursing home to my relationship with Leroy. After working there for only three weeks as a dishwasher, at the age of nineteen with no degree and no experience, I was hired as the activities director at Mother Hull Home. Word quickly spread that I could "talk" to Leroy. When someone on the staff needed something from him, they asked me to interpret. The man they'd thought obstinate and sullen proved to be amazingly agreeable once things were explained to him.

Leroy was one reason I was promoted, but another reason was surely my church affiliation. The administrator, an imposing woman with a deep voice, her steel gray hair cut close to her head, had come to Kearney, Nebraska, and Mother Hull Home by way of Alaska. She had a rugged, rough manner, and she walked a bit like a camel, throwing each large foot forward in slow, plodding steps. She and several of the members of the nursing staff were members of a conservative evangelical church, and the nursing home itself had been started and was still supported primarily by the Woman's Christian Temperance Union. Every month the board of directors for the WCTU, all elderly women, met in the dining hall. They always dressed up for the meetings, their white hair perfectly in place, wearing unostentatious suits and dresses, modest strings of pearls. They liked to see a Christian staff enforcing their rules: no drinking, no card playing, no dancing, no foul language.

Mother Hull Home was an interim care center, a facility mostly for patients who could not be on their own but didn't need extensive medical support. Most of the residents were poor and alone, their monthly bills paid through federal aid. Only a handful of residents required the sort of vigilant care common in other nursing homes, and the staff was especially fond of them.

I planned all the activities for the residents: art projects, lectures, music, readings, outings for those able. I organized volunteers and created seasonal and holiday decorations. I was also charged with keeping careful records for the state medical board. Among the things I was to administer was "reality orientation" to those patients who were suffering from "forgetfulness." I was principally charged with administering reality orientation with Nina.

Delusional and wheelchair bound, Nina stayed in her room

most of the time. She was afflicted with two powerful halluci-
nations, and these never varied in detail. Two huge, armed men
guarded the door to her bathroom—"There, don't you see them?"
The armed men irritated more than frightened her. They made it
impossible for her to use her own bathroom, forcing her instead
to walk across the hall to the public bathroom, which she tied up
for as long as half an hour at a time, always emerging after having
unrolled an entire roll of toilet paper into the trash can.

Under her bed was a baby she fretted over constantly. She
begged anyone who would listen to bring her milk for the poor
baby. "Can't you hear her? She's hungry." I knew Nina's problems
went well beyond forgetfulness, but the head nurse insisted I re-
mind Nina frequently what day it was. Each time I did this, it never
failed to arouse in Nina a look of such contempt and condescen-
sion I regretted it immediately. I eventually stopped the practice to
join some of the renegade nurses who conspired with Nina, and
more than once I sneaked a glass of milk to her room for the baby.

I disliked only one patient, a bitter woman named Ruth. She
had a permanent scowl on her face, and her voice was a perpetual
sneer. She came out of her room now and then to look disapprov-
ingly at our activities, muttering criticisms and complaints under
her breath. The food was terrible; the nurses were incompetent;
I planned ridiculous activities; the other residents were beneath
her; the whole place was abysmally managed. No amount of extra
effort on anyone's part appeased her. Otherwise, I remember the
residents with great affection. Blind Irene; the trio of sweethearts:
Violet, Ruby, and Anne; sad Elma, who had been abused by her
husband; Frank, whose one leg was perhaps six inches shorter
than the other, the sole of that shoe built up to allow him to walk;
August, who at eighty-eight had smoked since he was ten and was
proud of it and not about to quit now; Ed, who told me once that
when we died, we were dead like a dog—the first person I'd met

who didn't believe in an afterlife, shocking me with his matter-of-fact approach to death; Roy and his brother Gene, bachelor farmers who had lived together all their lives, both of them in their upper nineties. Neither of them had ever brushed his teeth. Never. And no amount of coaxing could convince them they should start. Their noxious breath filled their rooms, their tiny teeth yellow and gnarled like bits of broken corn, but still miraculously in their heads. They were both very dear, but I had to be careful not to get too close, especially to Roy, who was prone to grab and kiss. It happened only once to me, his foul lips sticking sickeningly to my cheek. Since he was hard of hearing, I developed a habit of standing just out of arm's length and leaning a bit to shout my message, primed to straighten up quickly if he so much as twitched.

I was glad to be out of the kitchen detail. In the three short weeks I'd worked with them, the kitchen staff had depressed me. Merna, the head cook, though a kindly older woman, had recently lost her husband and had been forced to leave their farm as a result. She was sweet, but her sadness was too much for me to bear.

The other two kitchen workers were both young women. One was Donna, a woman I compared to Elly May because of her golden hair and buxom figure and because she was none too bright. She was married to a much older man, who clearly saw her as his "baby doll," and when she repeated stories of their life together, Merna and I often exchanged troubled glances. Donna never seemed alarmed by her own life, but not so Tina, who was a bona fide half-wit married to an equally half-witted man, whose violence formed the core of most of her stories. Tina was aware of the trouble in her marriage, but her awareness did little to spare the rest of us graphic accounts of her horrible life.

That December, I left the job at Mother Hull Home to marry Gary—the man I'd met the year before at Bible college—and to move to Cozad, Nebraska. Before I left, the residents planned a going-away party and showered me with gifts they could hardly afford. I was filled with bittersweet emotion, for I knew I would miss them. Unlike so many of my friends who thought the rest home a depressing place, I had loved hearing the stories of the residents' lives. I left with the good wishes of all the elderly residents of Mother Hull Home, except Ruth, who during the wedding shower came out of her room one last time to sneer at all of us.

I had felt a little like a princess that day, being blessed by many loving fairy godmothers and fairy godfathers, when Ruth, like a dark fairy, seemed to curse me. "No matter," Irene had said. But a dark cloud had passed over our festivities, and afterward no one felt quite as merry.

IN COZAD, NEBRASKA, a hand-lettered wooden sign hangs across Highway 30 announcing to travelers they're crossing the hundredth meridian. The sign hangs on chains and blows in the wind. The hundredth meridian defines the point where the tallgrass prairie becomes short-grass prairie. This is where the West officially begins: the beginning of something and the end of something else.

Gary and I lived in a little gold house on Fourth Avenue. The young man who'd rented the house before us had curly red hair; and in the first few days I lived there, I frantically cleaned, trying to rid the house of what seemed like an infestation of red curls: in every crack and crevice of the bathroom, thick in the living room rug, and banked along the carpet's edge in our bedroom.

We had few furnishings—an antique Hotpoint stove we'd borrowed from Gary's grandmother, a gold refrigerator, a gray Formica-topped table with its four matching chairs, a twin bed we shared, and a small dresser. In the living room we had only two folding chairs and a good stereo system.

Gary was working for the rancher he'd been with for several years, and my mother-in-law had helped me get a job in the county treasurer's office where she worked, at the Dawson County courthouse. My father-in-law worked on the second floor of the courthouse as the director of the Dawson County welfare program. I rode to and from work with them every day.

That night late in January was dark and overcast. As we drove, weather reports warned travelers of a winter storm. The moon was a smudge of light filtered through the clouds, and an eerie blue light reflected off the snow still left on the ground from a storm the week before. A freezing mist made the highway dangerously slick.

In the car we were talking about a highly publicized murder trial then taking place in the county. Earlier that summer a woman had gone missing from her farmhouse near Cozad. Something about her disappearance had made local authorities suspect foul play, and they had mounted a massive manhunt. Men from across Dawson County and neighboring Lincoln and Buffalo counties gathered to search through area pastures for evidence of the crime. Confirming their worst fears, they found the woman's clothes tossed into a roadside ditch. Gary had been part of a search party nearby when a screwdriver stained with the missing woman's blood was discovered. It became the key piece of evidence linking the man now standing trial to the woman whose brutally tortured body was discovered soon after. The screwdriver had come from a factory in Lexington and had been easily traced to the suspect, a quiet, mild-mannered man, the Baptist minister's best friend. The suspect's wife had been with him in the courtroom every day, loyal still to the man she said had always been a good husband.

Six months before this murder occurred, another woman in the county had also gone missing under similar circumstances, only in that case no one had suspected foul play. Just that week, evidence in the murder trial suggested the suspect had likely murdered that woman too.

I'd learned before my wedding that the man for whom Cozad was named had also been a murderer. In light of this, the townspeople of nineteenth-century Cozad must have considered changing the name of the town, but Cozad it remained. Robert Henry Cozad (the son of the town's founder), however, had been so shamed by his father's crime that when the family left Nebraska after the murder, he changed his name simply to Robert Henri. He went on to become an artist and a founder of the Ashcan School.

Earlier that summer, while still planning our wedding, I developed a strange preoccupation. I didn't speak of it often, but the unalloyed joy I should have felt in my impending marriage had become tinged with sadness, fear actually, that it wouldn't happen, that Gary and I didn't have a future together. I blamed it on the terrible talk about that murdered woman and the violence of the town's founding.

As we neared Cozad that night, the mist turned to freezing rain, and our discussion in the car shifted to the irony of how the man whose wife had disappeared a year earlier had only two weeks before this come into the treasurer's office on the anniversary of his wife's disappearance to file for a divorce. He had finally given in to his worst suspicions that she'd simply left him without any sort of explanation. We wondered how he must feel now, as the murder trial that week had begun to hint she'd been murdered, too.

Visibility was very poor, and my father-in-law, always a careful driver, slowed to a creep. We all peered through the windshield as though our concentration could keep the car safely on the road and were relieved when we finally reached the town's outskirts. Through the haze of freezing rain while we waited to cross Highway 30, we saw the lights of an ambulance throbbing through the murk. We waited in silence as the ambulance passed.

"Bad night for accidents," my father-in-law said before slowly pulling through the intersection. He would know. For over twenty-five years he'd been an administrator in various county agencies that had made him privy to most of the bad news in the area. He was a bit obsessive when it came to safety. As a cautionary teaching tool when his kids were young, he'd driven them to see the sites of local car accidents.

I already knew more than I wanted to know about car accidents. My mother's sister, Janice, had been killed in a car accident six years earlier at the age of thirty-two, leaving four kids, ages seven through thirteen. More recently, in fact only three weeks before this, my mother's brother, Larry, also thirty-two, had been killed in an accident while driving his family—a wife and two young sons—home to Jamestown, North Dakota, after the Christmas holidays in Nebraska. He'd died instantly, his huge chest crushed by the car's steering wheel. At his funeral a few weeks earlier, I'd watched my aunt with a mixture of terror and admiration. I couldn't imagine how she was able to hold herself erect and graciously talk to other mourners.

My parents-in-law dropped me safely home, and I felt snug in my warm house as I started supper. I didn't know how to cook, but I was trying to learn. It was what I thought good wives did. I had a surprise for Gary that night, a blueberry cheesecake I'd made from a box and pork chops and rice. When I heard the front door open a few minutes later, I was puzzled. Gary always came in the back. I hurried to hide the cheesecake in the refrigerator so I could surprise him with it later. When I straightened to close the refrigerator door, I was startled to see my father-in-law, Ed, instead of Gary. It wasn't like Ed to walk into the house without knocking. He seemed distracted, his eyes searching the kitchen. "Is the stove turned off?" he asked, his eyes still not meeting mine.

"I have pork chops in the oven."

"Turn it off, and go get your shoes on," he said.

Without questioning him, I immediately did as he told me.

"Gary's been in an accident," he said after I returned to the kitchen. I stopped in the middle of the floor. My legs began to tremble, and I fell heavily into a kitchen chair. Although I managed to put on my shoes, my fingers shook so violently I couldn't tie the laces.

"Is he all right?" I finally asked.

"I don't know. We're going to the hospital right now." I stood up, immediately ready to follow him to the car. "Get your coat," he said, ever practical. I wondered how he could think of such details.

At the hospital my mother-in-law and Gary's youngest sister were already in the waiting room, its bright lights and colorful plastic chairs an affront to our dread. The slick magazines on the coffee tables seemed frivolous, insulting. Nurses and technicians hustled by us, pushing carts holding equipment, monitors, IV stands, and mystifying machines. I saw clearly they were dealing with a crisis. Occasionally I felt my stomach plummet. My skin felt chilled, and my extremities itched with anxiety. I kept getting up and pacing to the nurses' station, where every few minutes I tried to call my family. So far, I hadn't been able to reach them.

Later that night when the doctor finally came into the waiting room, he wrung his hands as he stood before us. He was the doctor who'd delivered Gary when he was a baby. He'd treated all his childhood injuries and illnesses. This man knew the body of the man I loved more intimately than I could ever hope to know it. My denial must have shown on my face, and at my hopeful expression, the doctor shook his head. "I just met you, and now I'm afraid I have nothing but bad news for you, Little Lady." He went on to explain Gary had died of a brain hemorrhage. He never regained consciousness after the accident. I stopped listening then, my mind frantic to hide from this new reality. I was convinced momentarily if I could only see Gary, talk to him, I could convince him to live again. When I suggested this, asked if I could see Gary, I was talked out of it. Soon after, we were shown to a back door, where we left to face the ice storm outside. Gary was gone that quickly, thrown from the driver's side door of his white VW Beetle after being broadsided by a car. He hadn't seen them for the mist. They couldn't stop for the ice. It was a bad night for accidents.

That night as I slept with my sister-in-law in her double bed, I woke again and again, each time knowing painfully and immediately the truth, not even having the luxury of a few seconds of forgetfulness.

The next morning I drove back through the icy streets of Cozad to the little gold house on 4th Avenue. The rooms were bitterly cold, and I found the thermostat had been turned down to fifty-five degrees. I guessed my father-in-law had returned to turn down the heat the night before. How odd, I thought. I packed a few clothes, made some phone calls to friends, grabbed the blueberry cheesecake from the refrigerator, and took it back to my in-laws' house, where sympathetic friends, neighbors, and church people were already gathering. I added the cheesecake to the sandwiches and casseroles, pies and cakes, Jell-O salads and vegetable trays, rolls and quick breads spread on the counters and tables to feed the gathering tribe. I had no desire to eat.

I couldn't stand to be alone, and I couldn't stand to be around people. I watched how everyone had a role to play, helpful or not—tragedy a community production. There was no room for idiosyncratic grief outside the choreography of coping traditions brought by these well-intentioned neighbors and the church community. Well meaning but misguided, kindly but stubborn, the community seemed to have answers for everything. They anticipated every doubt, every question. "It's not ours to ask"; "we don't always understand God's ways"; "it was meant to be"; "God's will is a mystery."

I bought it whole. Whereas, only days before the accident, I had been ready to leave the easy answers of organized religion and move on with my adult life, I now wanted nothing so much as to run straight back into the heart of it. Only the church had answers, I thought, for this sort of absurd calamity.

There were decisions to make, a funeral, flowers, songs, a hearse, a cemetery, a dinner in the church basement, preparation for the burial of a corpse that in no way resembled the man I had loved. I sat by the coffin and stared. Friends came. We laughed and cried and told stories. I was more exhausted than I'd ever been in my life. The thing was, I didn't only feel I had nothing, I really did have nothing. I lived in a town that wasn't yet my home. I lived in a rental house I would leave. I had a job I would give up. I had no plan for education or career. I had no insurance money. I would have to start over again. I was young, too young, and I'd been raised in a tradition that hadn't done much except encourage me to marry. I tried to console myself: I was fortunate not to have children depending on me; I didn't have a mortgage or any other debt; I was barely accustomed to the idea of being married. None of my reasoning, though, could disguise the blank space I saw as my future.

Pieces of me are still left there at the hundredth meridian, lost in spite of all my searching. I was still in love with a ghost, and I wanted nothing so much as to recreate my happiness. There would be no therapy or other counseling to help me. Faith was all that was needed. "I'm fine. Really, I'm fine."

And in this state, I began to make decisions for my future. Within a few months, I would move to Lincoln, the capital city, and share an apartment with my old friend Joy. There, I would meet again Ross M., who was now a graduate student at the university. This period was unavoidably a turning point. My life of faith had not prepared me for it. If I trace my later loss of faith to the fissure that resulted from my grief over Gary's death, it is also the site of my momentary return to faith, a blind, headlong, free fall back into organized religion, into a wrongheaded second marriage. Desperate for answers to define a life that had suddenly gone to sea, I found again, in my grief, my old familiar fervency, my passionate, zealous religiosity. I went mad in my own peculiar way.

March 2002

THIS IS THE THING. It's March. And at this moment in our life together, Noel and I are a bit at cross-purposes. I'm ready to have both time and money for other things. After raising children for more than twenty years, I'm ready to have fewer responsibilities. After the years of work and sacrifice to make the pink house what it is, every spare minute and every spare dime going toward that work, I want Noel and me to find another hobby we can enjoy together. Like what? Noel asks, very uncreatively, it strikes me. Ballroom dancing? I venture tentatively. Cooking? Travel? Jewelry making? A book club? He says the country house is his midlife crisis. He jokes that in lieu of a new sports car, or a girlfriend, or a new job, he wanted to change his life by tackling some big challenge. I'd glimpsed this restlessness in him before we found the country house, and I suspect it's true what he's saying. But this response feels a little flippant to me, and I'm not pacified by it.

I understand, and I don't understand. I don't know why his hobbies must always involve me to the degree they do. We're usually good about talking out our differences and reaching compromises without lingering resentments. We both agree the lack of resentment is the most astonishing thing about our marriage.

So. March already. And I was still worried that this house would become a decision I would resent, that I would never resolve my ambiguity and would eventually come to hold it against Noel. I know he feared this too. We were still monitoring our relationship to see if there was lasting damage.

So far I hadn't seen it. Not yet. But we had a fight in March. I was angrier with Noel than I'd ever been. Maybe my anger had been festering since December when I felt shut down that night at the restaurant. Maybe it had been festering since the 12th of September when we made the decision to buy the house in the first place. I couldn't say. In any case, Noel seemed unsurprised, seemed almost to have been waiting for it.

During the thirteen years of my previous marriage, I lived in a state of perpetual rage. I'd never been so angry and so frustrated in my life as I was in those years. It led to dramatic fights (on my side). I threw things. I used my sharp tongue mercilessly. I raged. In the end, I couldn't live that way. I hated myself in the relationship, hated what I'd become. So, it takes a lot for me to be angry now; all my fury seems to have been used up. And even when I'm really angry, it doesn't look like much. Our argument that night wasn't dramatic by anyone's definition. I was furious, though, and I said so. "I'm so mad at you." Noel, uncharacteristically calm, said, "I know you are." And perhaps I was disappointed by his calm response. Perhaps I wanted to have a more serious fight, but I couldn't if he wouldn't give me just a little more to work with.

I remember being enraged, feeling my blood pressure go up, and—my only reaction, so muted in comparison to the drama of the past—I stomped my foot. That's all I could muster. It felt good, though, and I did it again. It was late at night. Noel had been working all day and was relaxing now by playing a stupid computer game. I didn't care that he'd been working for fourteen hours and was exhausted.

When he still seemed unwilling to fight, I went back upstairs and seethed for a few more minutes. It wouldn't do. I needed to get something out of my system, and I went back downstairs and repeated the whole inane performance again. Noel didn't laugh. He didn't even smile. But beneath his calm I sensed he was slightly amused by my theatrics when I wanted him instead to be terrified or at least to take me seriously. But such expenditure of emotion is a luxury of a kind, and it was the sort of energy he didn't have at the time.

I stomped back upstairs, and this time I stayed there. We didn't speak again that night, both of us staying firmly on our own side of the bed. But somehow, inexplicably, when I woke in the morning, I wasn't angry anymore. I couldn't hang on to it. If I felt a grudge, it wasn't apparent to me the next day.

So far my ambivalence and sometimes frustration hadn't crystallized into rancor. If Noel still feared this possibility, in the same vein as his reply to me in December, he couldn't second-guess himself right now. He had to finish the job. I, however, was increasingly uneasy about what might be lurking in my heart. Unlike Noel, who always seems to know how he feels at a given moment, I often don't. My abrupt break with my past had come at a high price— a distance from myself and my feelings.

EVERY NIGHT for weeks now, when Noel came home, I soaked yet another load of his jeans, shirts, and socks overnight, hoping by morning enough of the drywall mud would have dissolved so they'd wash clean. At the country house, the mudding and sanding were still going more slowly than Noel had predicted, and it wasn't the comfort he'd anticipated it would be, as day after day it was all he did. In the end, our formula held true once more, as indeed the mudding stretched from three to six weeks. Despite Noel's earlier hesitation about Bob's help with mudding, he was again thankful for it as the job stretched on.

The only day I ever went to the country house alone during

construction was midmorning on a weekday in March to pick up a bag I'd left there the night before. A dense fog obscured the property from the road, and as I pulled into the drive, I was aware of how foreign the place felt. My discomfort quickly changed to something more akin to horror when, as I pulled into the drive, I saw perched on the granary roof five enormous vultures. I gasped out loud I was so shocked by their presence. The vultures weren't startled by me, and not one of them stirred even when I got out of the car. They were so close I could see their grotesque features clearly, and I felt as though they were there waiting for me.

I'm not usually so easily shaken, but the combination of the gloomy day and the squeamishness of approaching an empty house led me to interpret the presence of those birds in a distinctly macabre way. I knew I was being irrational, but I couldn't seem to shake the feeling as I drove back to town. For weeks after this, each time I pulled into the driveway of the country house, I braced myself, expecting to see those vultures peering down from the peak of the granary roof, even though they never again returned.

In the middle of the taping and mudding, our new kitchen cabinets arrived—three weeks in advance of when we had wanted them delivered. We had no place to store the boxes, and Lincoln Cabinet claimed they had nowhere to store them either. (Their explanation that their storage area was being used to house someone's car seemed flimsy to us.)

For days we brainstormed about what to do with the boxes. The granary leaked, so we couldn't risk storing them there. We were trying get the pink house ready to go on the market and didn't feel there was space for them there. Noel finally decided to rent a storage unit on the highway near Princeton and arranged to meet the truck and unload the boxes. Not only was this another evening of lost work, but because the cabinets arrived so far in advance of when we needed them, we wouldn't know until we opened the boxes weeks later if everything was as it should be.

Meanwhile, always having to think one or two steps ahead of the work, we'd been having an ongoing discussion about the big bathroom. I was leaning toward a more modern design, while Noel, who likes to soak after a long day at work, had his heart set on a claw-foot tub. We'd compromised with the idea of a platform tub, until we saw the exquisite five-and-a-half-foot, beautifully refurbished, vintage tub at Scherer's salvage. It was so impressive I had no difficulty changing my mind.

Mrs. Scherer may have been old, but she ran an amazing salvage business. All her fixtures, hardware, doors, and windows were stored impeccably and, in most cases, had been carefully refurbished. Despite being a good businesswoman, Mrs. Scherer was quirky. When she promised she could store the tub for a month after we bought it, in fact she couldn't. Shortly after the purchase, she began to call every day asking us when we planned to pick it up. My reminders to her that she'd agreed to store the tub for a month had been forgotten by the next day. After a week, her calls became more distressed, and we felt harassed. It was clear we'd have to find a way to store the tub as well as the cabinets. Unfortunately, there wasn't room in the small storage unit with the cabinets. Finally, Noel, with the help once more of the burly guys from the grain elevator, moved the tub into the granary where we covered it with an old carpet remnant and hoped it would be safe. We knew it wasn't a perfect solution, but at least Mrs. Scherer was no longer leaving distressed phone messages.

ON A SUNDAY near the middle of the month, our realtor, Jan, called me at the pink house. "I'm really sorry to bother you, but I have some buyers here from out of town who I think might like your house."

I glanced around, thankful I'd cleaned the day before. "Okay," I said hesitantly. I wasn't ready for this, and Jan knew it.

She continued, "Would it be all right with you if we stopped by in a couple of hours?"

"That'd be fine," I said, and even before I was off the phone, I was straightening the kitchen. In anticipation of putting the house on the market, I'd started to simplify, reducing some of the clutter, taking down personal photographs, and removing all the notes, clippings, and photographs usually tacked to the refrigerator. Now as I hung up the phone, I raced around the house, shoving into drawers and the backs of closets what I hadn't managed to put away earlier.

I was relieved I'd also cleaned the second story of the garage and the attic of the house, both of which had been given over to the kids through the years. The first time my father-in-law Floyd saw all the storage space at the pink house—an attic with deep built-in drawers and a large closet, in the garage a potting room and studio in addition to the two car stalls, and a large party room on the second floor—he'd warned us not to fill that space. We hadn't been able to imagine at the time how we could possibly fill it, but now, almost ten years later, it was indeed full.

Earlier in the month when I checked on the condition of the attics of both the house and the garage, I had to acknowledge the extent to which they'd also become catchalls for old furniture, toys, and building materials. In the attic of the garage, Finnegan had at some point unrolled and torn apart an entire roll of old insulation without my knowing it (and apparently without suffering any bad effects from the fiberglass he must have ingested).

I left the house later that afternoon just as Jan was arriving with a young couple. The woman was open and friendly, while her husband, a bit older than she, seemed guarded and uncomfortable at meeting me. They were planning an April wedding and moving to Lincoln from Kansas. He'd just taken a job with the Lincoln Public Schools. It was her first marriage, Jan told me later, and his second. He had two children from the previous marriage. I could see already in our brief encounter at the front door the man was leery of our urban neighborhood, and the woman, oblivious to the neighborhood, was smitten with the house.

I wasn't surprised when later that evening Jan called to report, "The woman fell in love with the house. She loved it that you had moved in the day after you got married." I was nodding as Jan talked, knowing what was coming next. "But the man is concerned about the neighborhood. He's worried about the schools."

Even though Jan couldn't see me, I was still nodding. "I'm going to write a little narrative," I said. "I'll describe this neighborhood." It wasn't necessary for me to continue, but as though I needed to convince Jan, I explained. "Our neighbors are wonderful. They were all here when we moved in. We're the first to leave. It's a very stable, safe place. I'll describe the lifestyle we have here."

"That's good," Jan said. "You should do that. To be honest, I don't think these were your buyers, but I still think you should go ahead and put the house on the market."

My shoulders sagged at this news. What if we were lucky enough to sell the house immediately and the new owner wanted to take possession in six weeks? Where would we go? Still, what if the market was tight and we couldn't sell? What if we had to make two mortgage payments? "All right," I finally said. "Let's do it."

Jan and Terry came over the following evening, and Noel cut his work short at the country house to be there to sign the papers. Months earlier, Terry had appraised the house for the bridge loan at a lower price than I felt we could reasonably ask. Noel was a little irritated by my insistence about this, but I'd persisted. Now, as the question of an asking price came up again, I said, "I really think we can ask more than you appraised the pink house for earlier." Terry nodded. I was prepared for him to disagree, but instead he said, "I think you're right." He went on to explain, "Before, we were trying to establish the base price, but I think the market is there for your asking price." Jan nodded.

"Listen," Terry went on. "Let's be honest. You could ask fifty thousand dollars more for this house if it were in another neighborhood . . ."

"I know," I interrupted. The neighborhood was hurting us, and our situation hadn't been helped when recently the *Lincoln Journal Star* had run a series of high profile articles on crime in Lincoln. Only the week before, a map had appeared on the front page of the newspaper highlighting what they called "high crime" areas. Our particular section of the Near South neighborhood was one of two neighborhoods singled out. Given the overall low crime rate in Lincoln, the articles seemed slightly ridiculous, but we knew the map would have a significant impact on the minds of potential buyers. Already we'd been asked by people who lived in suburban neighborhoods and had seen the articles if we weren't afraid to live in such a dangerous place. It had been easy to laugh at their ignorance before, but now we knew we'd be struggling against those flawed perceptions to get a buyer to even look at the property, let alone buy.

"There is a particular buyer out there," Jan said, as though reading my mind, "who will want this house *in* this neighborhood," and I loved her for understanding. As they left that night, I handed them the narrative I'd written about the life we'd enjoyed in the pink house with fond descriptions of all our neighbors.

"This is perfect," Terry said with his cheerful smile after he read it.

Before they left, I mentioned casually, "We have friends who said they might be interested in buying. I promised I'd let them know when the house went on the market." I shrugged. "I don't know what will come of it." My colleague Suzi, who had given me such good advice about lighting back in November, had mentioned to me a few weeks earlier that she and her husband, Nick, were thinking about buying for the first time. Suzi, who had been raised in southern California, loved midcentury modern design and had often expressed disappointment in not finding more modernist houses in Lincoln. Our traditional two-story prairie-style house with its deep front porch hadn't struck me as the sort of place she'd choose to buy. But Nick liked the pink house a lot. Both of them appreciated the neighborhood. That fact seemed crucial.

As I'd promised, the next day at work I told Suzi we were listing the house. Polite as always, she thanked me but didn't let on in any way what she was thinking. I sensed neither of us wanted to make too much of it and in no way wanted to create an awkward work situation.

AFTER WE BOUGHT the claw-foot tub, I spent many of my lunch hours scouring the antique shops in the Haymarket area for possible cabinets we could use to house the bathroom sink. Noel came during his lunch hours a few times to look with me. One patient antique dealer let us move several cabinets around in her store. I felt incredibly obnoxious doing it, and even worse when in the end we didn't buy from her. As she talked to us that day, she cheerfully told us stories about her farmer husband. "Cecil this and Cecil that." It was clear Cecil didn't share her taste for antiques, preferring instead to install new oak cabinets in their kitchen at home. She didn't shudder when she told us this, but she may as well have. She had a good sense of humor about Cecil, though it seemed obvious the shop was her way of being close to the things she loved but wouldn't allow herself to have at home because of Cecil. She found Noel a curiosity. "The ladies come in here," she said. "They love this stuff, but I don't see that many guys who do." She paused then. "I'd really like to see that house when you're done."

I formed my eclectic aesthetic during many years of living in poverty when my children were little, and I'd learned to be an adept scrounger. A seasoned thrift store shopper, I know how to turn other people's castoffs into something I find interesting. Forced by circumstance to adopt such tastes, I had liked shabby long before it became chic. I have a taste for squalor. Frankly, I was dumbfounded now by the high prices on primitive pieces I knew someone else had scavenged from the old barn, the chicken house, the basement, or the garage. Yesterday's junk was suddenly priced higher than fine antiques, and my taste had suddenly ceased to be practical.

In the end, we didn't find anything we felt would work in primitive cabinetry, and the big bathroom seemed to be stalled. Only by chance did that bathroom come together, when at the end of the month while buying fixtures for the shower in the small bathroom, we happened upon the first and only pedestal sink we'd seen with a base open to the floor, which we needed to accommodate the way our plumbing came into the addition through the slab. Noel stopped short when he saw it. He studied it silently for a while before finally saying, "I think this might work. I'll want to measure . . ." He craned his neck to look closer. "This could be our sink," he said. He looked at me. "Would you mind if the pipes showed a little?"

Thrilled, I said, "I don't care if there are some exposed pipes." The problem of finding a proper sink cabinet was alleviated, and the bathroom suddenly fell into place.

Suzi returned to the country house again. Always supportive and enthusiastic, she was complimentary about our progress. She must have noticed we'd incorporated her lighting suggestions. She surprised me before she left by telling me she and Nick had made arrangements with the Gabers to look at the pink house. I felt a little awkward, since as friends and colleagues we were suddenly in new territory. They'd be looking into our closets and behind our furniture, poking and prodding in ways far more familiar than I wanted to consider. Later, when we didn't back hear from Jan and Terry after Nick and Suzi's visit and Suzi said nothing to me at work, I was disappointed. Like the previous couple, I had to assume there was something about the house or the neighborhood they couldn't get past to make an offer.

Spring seemed to come overnight. One day snow, the next day green grass. At the country place the birds were like raucous children bursting through the door after school, all talking at once. Birds flew busily from tree to tree, as if in a panic to build their nests. Overhead, flying so high the V-formations looked like black threads, phalanxes of geese flew north. Despite the extreme distance above, their calls were still clear and distinct.

Spring in a cold place is always a hopeful time. The kids came out some weekends as the weather grew warmer and walked with me on the property. Their school year was coming to an end, and they were looking forward to summer. Jordan, who had been accepted into several good liberal arts schools, had in the end decided to enroll in the Honors program at the University of Nebraska, and she was happy with how her first year of college had gone. She and Leif were planning to move into an apartment together.

When they were younger, Noel and many of our friends had despaired for my kids. Given the circumstances of my divorce, their fears were often well founded. In spite of it all, though, the kids had grown into wonderful young people, responsible, funny, full of life. And maybe because of the struggles in their past, they're closer than a lot of siblings—good friends, in fact. On those walks with me they talked about their plans for the future, told me about their friends and their dreams. One thing was clear in every conversation. They planned to spend time at the country house.

House of Pain

I KNOW THE PRECISE MOMENT I should have left my second marriage and didn't. I know the time so well because at the foot of my bed was a large round clock with a thin band of black framing its face. Around the outside edge of the clock face were large numbers, perhaps two inches high, with distinct marks between each number to indicate the seconds. Across the face swept a willowy secondhand, passing each mark with an almost audible tick, a slight drag as it moved from second to second. The time was 2:03 A.M.

In fairness to myself I couldn't have left when I knew I should have because of the nurse who blocked my way. But then I'd summoned her. I'd been vomiting again, as I had been through the night, and she'd come to raise my head a bit to catch the nasty stuff in a kidney-shaped metal bowl. This wasn't ordinary vomit but a thin, yellow bile indicating the long time I'd gone without food. It burned my throat in a harsh acidic way. That night the metal bowl felt cold against my chin. I had a fever, and I trembled. Still feeling chilled as the nurse moved away, I asked for another blanket. She wasn't a bad nurse, just overworked and, having no time for small talk, didn't respond to my request. Based on her attentiveness throughout the previous eight hours, I trusted she'd eventually come back.

I'd been relegated to this recovery room after an experimental treatment, a regional chemotherapy, in which my leg had been attached to a heart/lung machine and the blood removed and mixed with mustard gas before being washed and returned to the leg again. The doctors hoped this treatment would arrest the progress of a serious malignant melanoma.

After what seemed like only a few seconds, I felt the curtain move aside. Assuming it was the nurse returning with the blanket and thinking it was awfully quick, I was ready to thank her, when I saw instead my husband, Ross. We'd been married only ten months. He grinned when he saw me and quickly pulled the curtain closed again. He told me how he'd been trying all that night to get in to see me but how there was a guard outside the recovery room door, some "guy with a rifle." Ross thought it was hilarious. "I almost got in earlier," he said. "But this guy stops me, says 'No one allowed past this door.' I thought, wow, they really guard this place. I didn't know what to make of it, but then I asked around and found out there's some South American diplomat just out of surgery."

I motioned with my head to my right. "In the next bed," I said. I wasn't very happy with the South American diplomat just then. He'd been restless since he'd gotten out of surgery a few minutes after me. I'd been awakened from a deep postanesthetic sleep to see someone thrashing against the curtain to my right. There'd been a scuffle as what sounded like two nurses and an assistant calmed the patient, who was swearing loudly in Spanish. I gathered from the exclamations of the two nurses that he'd pulled out all his tubes and, looking at the gear I was hooked up to, had marveled at his will: a catheter, oxygen, an IV dripping blood, another dripping glucose. I assumed he was hooked up to similar paraphernalia and hadn't been surprised to see a blood stain bloom on the white cotton curtain that separated our beds.

Now as I motioned toward it, I noticed the spot was still there, dried to a deep rust. That's how busy this place is, I thought; they haven't even replaced that curtain, which in some hospitals would be an intolerable admission of what really happens here, proof that this is about the spilling of bodily fluids, the making of sausage from people. I had clearly been in the hospital too long.

Ross was still grinning about his caper. I didn't ask why he was awake at almost 2:00 A.M. I didn't know then he'd spent the six hours I was in surgery running. Running? Why did that seem so strange to me, strike me as odd given the circumstances? Maybe if he were running to alleviate his stress, his worry. But no, there'd been none of that, only giddiness at being on an adventure, six weeks away from work to support his dying wife. He told me about the run at 2:02 A.M.

"I found this great trail, just a little way from the hospital." He gestured in the direction of the clock, and I wondered how on earth in this basement crypt he could possibly know his directions. I was looking at the clock as he spoke. "I had a terrific run, ten miles effortless. I'll be ready for the marathon with no trouble." 2:03 A.M.

But really, this is the story of my life—moments of crystalline perception followed by a sluggish indecision and an eager willingness to talk myself out of my own best interest, or by the interference of some well-meaning or ignorant person. In this case, it was the nurse, who'd returned, and, without a great show of it, without asking how he'd gotten into the recovery room, asked Ross to leave. Never losing that wide grin, his satisfaction at having accomplished his task earlier, he waved goodbye. The nurse tucked a warmed blanket around me, lifting the edges of the bed to secure it. I fell back into a drugged sleep. Do I remember now hearing that nurse whisper, "Fool," in Ross's direction after he left?

The first thing I saw upon waking again was the clock: 6:30 A.M. I'd been awakened by the sounds to my left of a woman being brought in from surgery. They start early around here, I thought. The woman—I'd glimpsed her before they pulled the curtain closed—had gray hair, flattened against the side of her head. On her face was still a trace of the orange iodine soap we'd all been doused in at the start of surgery. I learned later they poured a bucket of the stuff across the prone body of each anesthetized patient, later wiping off the patient's face with a rough towel, smearing, more than cleaning, before releasing us to the recovery room. I was still digging the soap out of the creases of my eyes, the corners of my mouth, the roots of my hair, the wells of my ears, the divots of my nose.

The new woman next to me was an amputee. I saw that too in the glimpse before the curtain—them hoisting her from the stretcher to the bed; one soft plump leg looking pale and vulnerable; an older woman in an undignified position; two young interns struggling with her weight; her bandaged stump jerking eerily. She was saying in a high-pitched voice, "Help me. Somebody help me." I guessed at first she was still not awake, in the distance of a strange dream, but for the next several hours she continued to repeat this plea. She was crying too, and the nurses came frequently. She flailed; she complained about pain, not in the stump but in the phantom limb. The bottom of her foot, the one that didn't exist, had a terrible cramp. The nurses told her soothingly this was normal, tried to calm her with drugs. I lay awake and listened and watched the seconds tick by, that brief catch with each tick. Mercifully, the South American diplomat was sleeping. I guessed this only because he was now silent.

Our beds were lined against one wall in a large narrow room. White walls, a white industrial tile embedded with gold flecks, metal beds, white sheets and blankets, and white cotton curtains hanging on metal rods with metal clasps separating the many beds, so that in the otherwise quiet room was the frequent grating sound of metal sliding against metal. There was the occasional sound, too, of people groaning, retching, crying. The curtains extended to the foot of each bed, leaving open the remainder of the room, which served as a corridor along which nurses—wearing the traditional whites and in this case even those old-fashioned nurses' caps—walked soundlessly in their soft-soled shoes, though now and then a shoe squeaked on the waxed floors. At the foot of my bed, framed in the white wall, was the clock I've described. I kept craning my neck trying to see beyond the end of my curtain, hoping to glimpse a window, even a small casement, in this dreary place where the lights were never dimmed. I needed the reassurance of the sun rising to believe the clock on the wall: 7:30 A.M. I saw no windows.

All surgical cases were required to stay in this recovery room for twenty-four hours. It felt like a prison sentence when I realized I wouldn't be leaving until 6:00 P.M., no matter how well I felt.

IT WILL NOT BE TRUE if I say I married this man because he once found an injured sparrow. He kept the sparrow in a box with a bit of blanket, while he nursed it back to health. If I tell that story, then I must also tell how that same bird was later killed by his negligence, smothered by an old woman whose name really was Fanny Butz and who unwittingly sat on the bird he'd let out of the box. I don't know why he took the crippled bird out of the box and put it carefully in an overstuffed chair in a house where he was staying— Fanny Butz's house. Since the bird could neither fly nor sing to protect itself, it had no way of warning the old woman, who, both short of sight and poor of hearing, couldn't possibly have seen the bird before she sat down, and never did. To his credit, he never told her what she'd done. I think I tell the story with this twist because that's how he represented himself at the time, the hero for having not embarrassed Fanny Butz, never taking any responsibility for having left a helpless thing in an inappropriate place unattended. This is how the truth keeps moving past me.

I could explain how one night this man, my husband, helped

three men in trouble, gave them a place to stay. It was a cold winter night, and the three men would otherwise have been sleeping in their car. "Or the City Mission," I'd suggested. "They could stay in the City Mission." But I was being difficult because this was about him being helpful, being generous, helping three men down on their luck. He brought them home for a meal, tomato soup okay? Grilled cheese? I played my part even though there were no groceries in the house. I'd just given birth to Leif six weeks earlier. Both the baby and I were sick. Later that night Ross would leave for work, a strange job in the middle of the night loading trucks for UPS, after which he would take graduate classes at the university where he was finishing a PhD. From 2:00 A.M. on, the baby and I would be alone with these three strange, down-on-their-luck men.

But actually, it didn't happen that way, because that night I left, for the sake of the baby if not for myself. The next afternoon Ross came to get us at my sister's house while my sister and her husband watched nervously, wondering no doubt what I would do. I did nothing. There was no scene, no tantrum, no harsh words. I simply bundled up the baby and myself and went back. But I don't want to tell this story. I want to describe instead the hospital, where I was before the baby, before the three strange men, when I first knew what I needed to do and didn't.

There were waiting rooms everywhere and little offices and labs off narrow winding hallways like a prairie dog town. The sensation was distinctly subterranean. I had the feeling, too, that rooms had been added quickly, halls narrowed and space divided without much of a plan, as though there had been a catastrophe of some sort requiring this hospital suddenly to provide twice as much of everything as it had at one time. There was a spirit there, too, of a place in midtrauma, the site immediately following a disaster. This description of the hallways, the badly designed additions, the spirit of frenzy, is a way to avoid telling about the people I saw in those waiting rooms: men without faces, women missing noses or one of their eyes, all kinds of amputations, children without hair with large hematomas on their skin.

The chairs were much too close together in the waiting rooms, exacerbating the offensive smells; perfumes and colognes and soaps couldn't mask the smell of antiseptic, institutional disinfectant, rubbing alcohol, urine, sweat, putrid sores. I see still the immaculately dressed woman without an arm, a long sleeve meant to disguise her amputation, expensive gold jewelry to further distract attention. She and her husband were from France, wealthy enough to come to this clinic for their last chance at hope.

And the Italian man called Zeppi by his large family, all of whom had come with him to stay while he was being treated for a rare form of bone cancer, bringing with them each day amazing Italian meals they shared, having taken a liking to me. I could never figure it out until I saw Zeppi's mother looking at me one day as she spoke in Italian to her daughter-in-law, Zeppi's wife. "Bella," she said and then shook her head. A child. I'd just turned twenty-two. They, like me, believed I was dying. The entire extended family had been living in the hospital's temporary housing for more than a year. From the first moment I met Zeppi, though, I saw beneath his enthusiastic smile, his strangely accented "Everything's okay," he was a dead man. Only now do I confess I kept my distance because of it. I said boldly to him then, "I won't make my death my life." I intended to go home, to take my chances, once this particular treatment was over.

The mix of languages in those rooms was not as exotic as might be expected. It clashed terribly with the smells and the something else that made this crowd unlike any other crowd I've ever waited with. This was not the crowd waiting for a movie to start, waiting for a ball game to begin, waiting in line to return the broken toy after Christmas, waiting for the curtain to open on a stage. When people ask those theoretical questions like whether emotions have colors, I know they do. This color was brown. Suffering is brown.

Why should I mention putrid smells and people missing vital parts, especially faces? Why should anyone need to know I lived in a wheelchair for months, and for months after that walked with a cane, and for the months following that, walked slowly with pain and with each day felt joyful I could walk at all? Why should anyone need to know there's a fine line to negotiate between a healthy acceptance of what appears to be an inevitable death and the desire to live? These are perhaps things not to concern myself with. Except this is a metaphor for other types of negotiation, like marriage, for instance.

I can't seem to look at anything straight on anymore, and that's part of the problem. Somewhere much later there was a court battle, and I was on trial to determine whether I was a good mother or not. I remember wanting to laugh, thinking it can't be true that they expect me to answer yes or no. Were you a good mother? Show me the good mother, I wanted to say. I wanted to enumerate my weaknesses, like this was some sort of confessional, like this was about divining the truth, because that's how I am. I wanted to discuss definitions and social constraints, gender contracts and role playing. At heart I'm a philosopher, which I now understand has no place in the courtroom, maybe no place anywhere.

It goes back to the waiting room in that cancer hospital where people are missing parts. I can't pretend I haven't seen the human body dismembered, a terrible indignity, but I understand its multiplicity better than I did before. I understand that there are a number of ways to be alive, a broad spectrum that separates the living from the dead, that there are no such poles as good and bad.

I didn't leave my husband at 2:03 A.M. that morning, and by 9:30 A.M. I'd forgotten my clear resolve of the night before. The South American diplomat was awake and acting up again, not, as he had in the night, pulling tubes from his body, but swearing and barking orders again in Spanish. I decided he was insufferable.

I looked at his bodyguard standing at the foot of his bed where he'd stood through the entire night. I noticed the revolver in his belt, his stoic uniform, his hat—he was wearing a hat, for god's sake—and I thought if I were him, I'd shoot that white-haired Spanish sonuvabitch right between the eyes. I realized even then this was post-op depression speaking. I could understand that by 10:30 A.M., and, of course, it helped that the diplomat had calmed down again. I liked him much better when I didn't have to hear him.

I knew his hair was white—thick, and wavy, and white—because earlier, for some reason, a nurse had pulled the curtain between our beds back for a second. The diplomat and I had locked eyes briefly before he looked away. I had a moment's satisfaction as I noted how his white hair had been stained orange around the edges with the sticky iodine soap. He may have been a diplomat in South America, but here in the sausage factory we were all the same. I wondered if he was from Rio de Janeiro, where they were shooting street children like you might vermin, where when they talk about cleaning up the city, they mean murdering these children who make it bad for everyone else. Tens of thousands of them. I was in a bad mood, and my head itched with that same iodine soap.

Earlier that morning when I'd awakened, I'd been hot, burning up, and had counted seven blankets over me, their ends all tucked tightly under the mattress. I'd peeled off a few layers, but I hadn't wanted to go too far. I didn't want to see what they'd done to me. Each time the nurse came to check, said she was "just going to take a peek," lifted the blanket and prodded about, I turned my head away. That's okay, I thought, I'd rather not see. I wasn't curious in the least about mutilation, especially when it was mine.

The catheter burned and itched. I felt an intense pressure on my bladder before a strange, unpleasant emptying sensation when the nurse lifted the bag. I didn't want to look too closely at anything here, how someone else's blood had been dripping into my arm all night. I'd had two pints already, and in a brief conference earlier the doctors had decided to give me more. I didn't want to know why I'd lost so much blood.

There is the memory, always, of that other hospital, a time when I was still healthy. I'm haunted still by the words of the doctor, "I just met you, and now I'm afraid I have nothing but bad news for you, Little Lady." I remember I wanted to laugh when he called me Little Lady. I could still be amused by things. You don't tell someone the man she loves has died by saying it's nothing but bad news, do you? I wouldn't have thought so. Bad news seemed to suggest to me it wasn't great news, but it wasn't the end of the world. That's what he should have said. "Little Lady, I have to tell you, this is the end of the world." Then I would have known. I would have been prepared.

Later, that same night, we left by a back door. It seems strange now, being shown the back way, as though they hadn't wanted anyone in the clean, bright emergency room to see us grieving. From this gesture I'd concluded hospitals didn't like death, weren't comfortable with it, until I found myself in this clinic where death was an everyday, walking-around reality. A place where you came to die. On that other night, though, as we walked out the back exit, through which only hours before they'd brought Gary's body on a stretcher, I saw on the floor in front of me the clothes he'd worn that day, dropped where they'd been hastily cut away. Cold air startled me as the door opened into the darkness after our long night of waiting.

They hadn't let me see him. I was young, and I hadn't known to insist. I've heard people can still hear, that hearing is the last sense to leave us. I've wondered if I couldn't have talked him back across the bridge that night—for that's how I'd pictured it then, a bridge between life and death—asked him not to leave. I've wondered if maybe he was waiting to hear my voice, straining to hear it above the urgent and unfamiliar voices of the ER. Maybe he took my silence as disinterest. I looked down that night after the blast of cold air and noticed my shoelaces were untied. In my haste to get to the hospital I'd forgotten to tie my shoes. Insignificant detail. Those seem to be the only ones I recall.

MY STAYING IN THAT SECOND MARRIAGE for twelve more years sometimes can feel like those twenty-four hours spent in the basement recovery room of a big cancer research hospital, where surgeries are handled in mass production; where bodies float through time and space from one laboratory to another for one test or another, from surgery to recovery, with bureaucratic efficiency; where there is no illusion of free will, and time ticks away in front of your eyes while you're forced to wait, kept from those you know, and you avoid looking at the obvious erosion of the self as you thought you knew it; where you pine for what you once had and find in its absence a singular pain.

But I can't leave it there, on such a sour note, such a despairing analogy, for it's not like that at all. There is a happy ending, there really is. Time passes. We endure. We survive even when we've been told it's not possible. Sometimes we beat the odds. And after a while, a time far away from that 2:03 A.M., I did leave. It was no easier leaving then than it would have been to leave that well-guarded hospital with a bum leg and a bad prognosis and two armed guards protecting a mad diplomat, but I did eventually leave. And with time I've also learned this lesson: gratitude is the sum of what you have lost and in some way found again.

April 2002

BEFORE I COULD CONCEIVE of leaving my second marriage, I first had to leave the faith that had for so long kept me captive. I had been a precocious believer. By the age of five, I was singing solos in church, and at six I was baptized by immersion. Because the individual must choose to receive this form of baptism, which the Christian Church believes is essential for salvation, my parents had doubts at first that my six-year-old mind had grasped the enormity of the decision.

In the stark landscape of my ranch upbringing were no neighbor children. No parks. No museums. It was an austere place where I grew up with my loving and nurturing family. But I was a child who wanted to sing and dance, to play the piano, to make up stories and plays, to draw elaborate pictures of mythical worlds. Where else in that environment but the church would I have found the sort of beauty I craved? Only the church provided music and color and words. Such beautiful words. I hear still the words I first heard with chills at a Christmas pageant when I was very young, "And lo, this night in the city of David a son is born, Christ the Lord." And the Old Testament stories: such passion and commitment. Such spectacular human folly and sin. Sin. I understood well the salvation I was receiving by going under the baptismal water at age six. I was making a choice for a grander life.

In many ways I wasn't disappointed. I had a grand interior

life. Perhaps I wouldn't have lost my faith if I'd been born into a church tradition that hadn't demanded such literalness of belief, if I'd been exposed to the silent ritual of liturgical worship. Instead, I was privy to the sermon, to the Sunday school lesson, where no story was valued or recognized for its symbolic content. Or perhaps a Pentecostal faith with its emphasis on the gifts of the spirit, allowing for a quirky individual vision, might have been enduring for me. But even as I seem to mourn my lost faith, I know it is irrational. Still, there are things I miss.

I miss my former fundamentalist friends. The camaraderie of shared assumptions, the likes of which I'll never find again, is worth a moment of affectionate nostalgia now and then. There was real community with those friends. Every weekend we met to cook meals together, take long walks, watch movies, listen to music, and talk. We talked long into the night. If through the years my ideas became more and more abstract, more mystical, even dangerously ecumenical, and if now and then I alarmed my friends with these ideas, I was still one of the gang and my house a central meeting place. Those conversations, I now recall, spiraled and billowed. Ideas blossomed and stacked gloriously, airy and high. Such conversations reflected an intense search for the truth I no longer pursue. The truth I found took me straight out of the very group that had provided such fertile ground for that work.

One night shortly before I finally left the church, I remember telling one of my friends I wanted to know myself so well I would be perfectly distilled, "like a drop of water, know exactly who I am in any circumstance," while at the same time "so big, so capable of understanding anything human that like an ocean I could find room for everyone and every idea." "You want to be God?" my friend said critically that night. I hadn't thought about it that way, that paradox a perfect description for what some might call God. "Why not?" I answered.

And then I read Blake, "Everything that lives is holy." And the

Tao-te Ching and Jung and Freud. This was no crisis of faith. Rather, it was an ever-expanding acceptance of broader truths. I'd always been a part of the religious left, concerned about human rights and economic fairness and frankly alarmed by the church's increasing obsession with social issues that felt intrusive and dangerously distracting. In the end, leaving the church wasn't at all as big a leap as I'd imagined.

It was about this time I had a dream. In the dream I had come into an old-fashioned college classroom. I was late for class, and everyone else had left. There'd been a test that day, and the professor, an old white-haired man, who showed no impatience with my tardiness, pointed to where I should start. The test involved a number of booths at which a series of mathematical principles were enacted. My task was to name the principle or the theory behind the illustration. This was *not* a math class, and as I went from booth to booth, my test paper blank, I grew angrier and angrier. Finally, in complete frustration, as I at last put the unfinished test on the professor's desk, I began to cry. The professor and I seemed to have a friendly or familiar relationship, and he came from behind his desk to hug me in a fatherly way. He seemed genuinely concerned as he tried to comfort me, but I pulled away from him in anger and said, "If I fail, you fail too." The meaning seems clear. I was telling the God I'd created—a kindly, delusional, and ultimately cruel God—goodbye. I sometimes miss him too.

Despite feeling less burdened now that I've laid my faith aside, I'll confess I feel life is less magical, less intensely personal, too. While I had faith, I felt I was the center of a meaningful drama, part of the vital fight over my soul. The universe had a specific beginning and a prescribed end. There was a definite plot—a war between good and evil that would inevitably end in a violent and glorious battle with the good guaranteed to win. No action film could compete with my own psychodrama. Trumpets would sound. Every knee would bow. All tears would be dried, and peace would reign among all things. Beautiful words. "There will be no more crying, no more tears."

My faith was like a thick curtain, like a flat-earth theory of the world. I felt safe and knowing within its parameters. I'd sometimes ventured close to the edge or reached out to pull back the curtain, but in the past, I'd always retreated to the safe world of my beliefs. Paradoxically, the sense of clear boundaries allowed me this freedom of range. I had a sense of knowing where I was in the world.

Now, with all sorts of intellectual freedom, I often find my world is strangely prescribed. Though the world seems more vast, I opt not to explore it as much. So little is at stake now. While my faith had limits, those limits became the site of great intellectual work, defining, defying. Despite what my nonbelieving friends think, many of my fundamentalist friends were (still are, I trust) smart, interesting, educated, well read. I would still find many conversations with them stimulating and challenging, but I gave up my passport to that world. I had to. And even as I miss that sense of belonging, it's in much the same way that I miss childhood. There's no going back.

It wasn't easy to leave. I'd been warned all my conscious life about "out there," "the darkness," "the unsaved," "Satan's sphere of influence." The books that might have introduced reason or moderation into my life when all this fervor first began in adolescence were somehow never available. They weren't on the bookshelves at home, and in my school's curriculum the often archaic reading material somehow never cut through the bulwark of my already captive imagination. I'd like to say I was looking for something in my adolescence and never found it, but truthfully, I had developed a resistant arrogance. It was *I* who was privy to information others needed; *I* who knew the truth; *I* who had the key to salvation. What could penetrate such suspicious overconfident armor as that? The changes had to come slowly from within myself.

Along with a sense of belonging in my faith community, there was at the same time a keen awareness of being an outsider, of being part of a submerged group, isolated and confined, far from the dominant culture around us. I wasn't aware enough of what I was missing to be someone who, as Yeats once said of Keats, had her "nose and face pressed against the sweetshop window." Instead, I would later find my own experience better mirrored by that of Wallace Stegner, who, like me, had grown up in geographic and intellectual isolation and who believed no amount of education or experience could quite close the resulting gaps.

NOW, THOUGH, YEARS LATER, as we prepared to put the pink house on the market, I felt so far away from my former life, my former self, that my own past sometimes felt like someone else's story.

We scheduled the listing date for April first. Jan and Terry had a spare key and knew how to crate Finnegan should they need to show the house while we were away during the day, and we were all aware of the need to leave the house tidy each morning. We were as ready as we would ever be.

That last weekend in March I finally told all our neighbors so they wouldn't be shocked by the For Sale sign in the yard come Monday. It had been hard to tell them we were leaving and harder yet to explain we didn't want to leave the neighborhood so much as to have the experience of living in the country.

The neighbors were all kind, though obviously disappointed, as the kids and I went from house to house with the news. In an urban neighborhood like ours, there was always the fear a house would be bought and turned into apartments. Often poorly managed, these properties had for years threatened to destroy the integrity of the Near South neighborhood.

We thought we'd kept the project a secret from everyone, but during these visits, I discovered the Hatch family across the street from us already knew. They'd heard about the country house a few months before from a mutual acquaintance and had discreetly not mentioned it.

The Sunday night before the house went on the market, everything was as orderly as I could make it, and we prepared ourselves to have a good attitude as in the weeks ahead strangers trooped through. As I was cleaning earlier in the day, I looked out the windows and noticed it had started to snow. The snow continued all day, and by evening a rare spring blizzard raged outside, a perfect April Fools' eve. I felt a little let down that this was the way the house would go on the market.

Already a foot of snow had fallen when at 9:00 P.M. the phone rang. It was Jan. "Could you and Noel come out to the office? We've just had an offer on your house."

"You're kidding." I glanced out the kitchen windows at the drifts in our yard. "Tonight?"

Jan laughed softly. "Nick and Suzi have been here since five drawing up the proposal, and they're ready to make an offer."

I covered the mouthpiece of the phone and relayed the information to Noel.

"Wow!" he said. What else could he say? After all our preparations, we hadn't expected anything like this, and the blizzard outside made it seem a little surreal.

"We'll be there in an hour," I told Jan before hanging up the phone. Their office at Woods Brothers was halfway across town from us, and we drove slowly through the empty streets of Lincoln in Noel's Chevy, thankful again for the four-wheel drive, as most of the streets were still unplowed. It took us forty-five minutes to make the trip. Remembering the late night in September when we'd made our offer on the country house, I wondered briefly if all real estate deals took place at 10:00 P.M.

"These are your buyers," Jan said in a whisper as she opened the door for us. "It's the sort of neighborhood they want, close to the university, diverse. They know exactly what they're getting here." There was no one in the office but the six of us, and as in all large buildings when they're empty, our voices seemed to echo in the cavernous silence.

We'd heard nothing from Nick and Suzi since they'd viewed the house, so we were surprised but elated by their offer, especially coming now on the eve before the house went on the market. Instead of the For Sale sign I'd promised the neighbors would be a big orange Sold sign in front.

After we accepted the offer, we waited a bit nervously to hear when they wanted to take possession.

"Actually," Nick said. "I'm leaving for England in May and won't be back until the first of August." I panicked thinking they'd want to get into the house before Nick left.

"We have to be out of our apartment before the first," Suzi added, as if thinking aloud. Finally, she concluded, "End of July would be the best time for us to take possession."

At this, my heart skipped a beat in relief.

"So would we postpone the closing until then?" Noel asked.

Terry glanced quickly at Nick and Suzi then back to us. "Nick and Suzi would like to lock into their loan as soon as possible because of the good rates right now."

Jan went on to explain. "Maybe the four of you could sit down sometime and work out the terms for a rental agreement."

"That's a perfect situation for us," Noel said.

Our official closing on the pink house was scheduled for April 29, six months to the day after we'd closed on the country house. We'd begin paying rent in the amount of Nick and Suzi's mortgage payment from the first of May through July 24th.

Later, although I admitted to Noel I was relieved the pink house had sold so quickly and was comforted by the thought that within the month we'd no longer be responsible for two houses, I felt that night a sliver of sadness, knowing now there was truly no turning back. We were committed to leaving the pink house.

NOEL FINALLY FINISHED the dry walling in April. Weeks and weeks of doing the same sort of work with no end in sight had made both of us once more seriously question whether we could reasonably finish the project on schedule. Now, though, it wasn't only the specter of the inspection we needed to pass but our own need to have a place to live in July. Since I no longer had to worry about showing the house, I began to pack. Noel's parents, Floyd and Marie, came again. Marie packed all the dishes in our large dining room sideboard and buffet, as well as the dishes in the upper kitchen cabinets. I began to make a triage: boxes to get rid of, boxes to sell, and boxes for the new house. Leif and Jordan had made plans to get an apartment together, so whatever we couldn't use and the kids thought they might need was set aside for them.

Floyd planned to stay on for a couple of weeks more to help hang the kitchen cabinets and lay the ceramic tile. Noel scheduled a Sunday when Tracy from the grain elevator could join them to help with the cabinets. I was excited to finally see the kitchen start to take shape. Marie went with me to watch their progress that Sunday, so we were there when Noel opened the boxes and discovered the manufacturer had failed to send a base for the bottom corner cabinet. This was no small oversight. The bottom corner cabinet was the cornerstone for successfully hanging all the other cabinets, and this omission brought their work to a complete standstill as Noel spent the better part of the day gathering materials and building the missing base. Given his trouble in finding a time when Tracy was available to help, Noel was especially incensed about this mishap.

I'd seen how angry he was when he first found the problem, but the fact that he was still angry later that night when he and

Floyd came home surprised me. "You just can't find good products or good work," he said to me later. "I don't get it. What if we'd hired installers? They aren't carpenters. They would have had to hire someone to come out and build that base." He paused and grumbled under his breath. "Who's going to compensate me for my labor and lost time?" What could I say? He was right. But this had always been the risk with this project. We'd known all along there would be surprises, disappointments, unexpected costs. Noel hadn't allowed himself, so far, to get too bogged down by the various curves he'd been thrown, but his acute disappointment in the poorly executed work of skilled labor and in poor product quality got to him in ways nothing else could.

In the days to follow, Noel and Floyd managed to hang the cabinets by themselves. The bottom cabinets were all installed by the time I got to the house again, and despite Noel's frustration with how things had gone, I loved them. I felt enormous relief in seeing finally the outlines of the kitchen I'd imagined.

By the end of the week, however, when the cabinets were all installed and Noel hung the cabinet doors, there were further disappointments as he discovered the pantry doors were badly warped. They'd been shimmed out to almost a half an inch at the top. In addition, one of the pantry pullouts had a loose bottom. Lori, at Lincoln Cabinet, was responsive to Noel's call, though, and immediately contacted the factory. I was reminded then of my reasoning in December not to get cabinets from one of the discount stores for fear of exactly this situation.

Floyd and Noel turned next to the backbreaking job of laying the ceramic tile. Working on their knees for hours, both Noel and his dad were sore and exhausted when they finished each night. I hadn't yet seen the tile laid, but Noel had been coming home each evening with dire reports. Now that it was being laid, he didn't like the color. It seemed greasy looking to him, yellow rather than gray, the pattern no longer interesting but overpowering.

Because of these reports, I delayed going out to the house for a couple of days. When I finally saw the tile, I felt sick. It was the first decision we'd made in the house that I thought was a serious mistake. And unfortunately, it was a big one since there was no way we could tear up all the tile they'd laid. We were going to have to live with this mistake for a very long time.

Noel and I didn't have the heart to say any of this to Floyd, but we were deeply discouraged. The extent of my disappointment wasn't entirely evident to me until, a couple of weeks after I'd first seen it, I woke in the middle of the night stewing about the tile. I realized then that the biggest problem wasn't only the tile itself but how it limited our choices for wall color. I realized I needed to resign myself to the fact and to work *with* the tile rather than compete with it. The paint choices would need to be more monochromatic than I'd hoped, the wall colors pulled out of the tile.

And even as I was consumed with solving problems of this sort, I couldn't help but be shocked by the banality of it all, making such paltry decisions post-9/11, putting such effort into relatively insignificant decisions, while every day in the publishing house where I worked, I was making decisions of far greater consequence and stewing only a little more about them. Somehow, though, in the feverish context of this project, these materialistic and often shallow-seeming decisions were moved to the forefront in my mind; and I needed to solve them in ways I could live with, since the house would represent a significant part of my life.

We'd already been debating about the style of this house, and in many ways, the tile fiasco helped us make a decision we'd been putting off. We decided to opt for simplicity and conformity. Interest would have to be created through furnishings, rugs, and wall hangings, not through elements of the structure or paint colors. Because the floor plan was open and because we weren't working with any original architectural details except the fir floors, we began to conceive of the house as simple, modern, and spare, rather than our usual quirky, eclectic style. We proceeded to order six-panel doors to be used throughout. There would be no more discussions about paint or stain. We'd paint the doors and wood-work. White walls and white woodwork in all the rooms with wood floors and in the bedrooms. What I liked to call a latte color on the walls of the entryway, the hallway in the addition, and the little bath, and a dark gray-brown in the big bath, above the wainscot. "Rodent colors," as a friend later called those gray-browns. All the hardware would be brushed nickel.

NOW WITH SPRING, responsibilities outside the house competed for attention with those inside. The sewage lagoon is a beautiful system of waste-eating microbes, but its simple elegance depends on sunlight and air to keep the microbes alive. Our lagoon, like everything else on the property, had been badly neglected, and the same volunteer trees and aggressive tall weeds prevalent on other parts of the farmyard were well established there. I spent a pleas-ant April day cutting out the most egregious offenders. It was by no means the cleanup the area needed, but it was a start.

In addition to birdsong, we'd been hearing the sounds of frogs, and as I worked near the lagoon, there they were, hundreds of them, their tiny heads coming out of the algae-topped surface, singing their hearts out. As if on cue, they all grew silent at the same time, then submerged themselves for several seconds before beginning again. Each time they resurfaced, I had to smile at their earnest song and the silliness of their habitat.

Through the early years when Ingrid lived on the property, she'd been an active gardener, fencing off numerous places for her various flower, vegetable, and herb gardens. We guessed that af-ter her divorce she'd let the place go. Already by the end of April, the grass was turning green, and the weeds were coming back.

Mowing early, we knew, would help control the weeds we'd seen when we'd first visited the place in September. Before we could mow, though, it was my responsibility to take down the yards and yards of old fencing Ingrid had put up around the property and to remove the steel T-stakes holding the fence in place.

My sister Tami and her husband Kent came to help. They lived in western Nebraska and hadn't seen the house before this. Tami is a professional photographer, and I knew as she looked around she was scoping out photo ops. Kent is a judge. His resistance to being defined as "the honorable" was always evident in his T-shirts, jeans, shaved head, and goatee. He had long dreamed about living in the country, and as he worked that day—single-handedly pulling T-posts out of the hard, clay soil—he seemed happy in a way I hadn't seen him in a long time. That afternoon they helped me remove at least fifty old T-posts and enough fencing to fill the back of the pickup and a trailer behind it.

With all the mowing we'd be doing, we knew we'd need a riding mower of some kind, and Noel had found, earlier in the month, an old Montgomery Ward lawn tractor with a mower and a snow blower attachment complete with snow chains. It was a machine, a solid piece of cast iron, and he was pleased, now that the fencing was gone, with how it moved through the grass. We still couldn't mow some areas because of old foundations from former farm buildings. In the future we'd have to bring in a backhoe to get rid of the rubble in those places.

For now, though, we were happy winter was past and we could sit in the yard and listen to the birds and the frogs, smell the spring air, and dream about the day when we'd be finished with our work. Our thoughts, like those of most midwesterners this time of year, also turned to the garden. In the fall we'd already been thinking about where we might plant the vegetables. Not surprisingly, between the two of us it is Noel who is the skilled gardener, but I have an innate sense of the worth of a garden and come from a long line of great gardeners.

My fondest memories of both my grandmother and my father have to do with their gardens. It's always seemed fitting to me that they both died in April. My father had died ten years earlier in his garden, a heart attack killing him while he was preparing the ground. He died literally with a hoe in his hand. And my grandmother died five years later after a year-long battle with cancer, the only spring in her long life when she didn't plant a garden.

My father's gardens were eccentric. He cared little for conventions of gardening and preferred experimenting to cultivating perfection. His gardens were comical, erratic, and fecund; only he knew completely the logic of the plot. My grandmother, by contrast, was orderly, her rows clearly marked. She allowed no disruptive castor bean plants among the tomatoes; the beets were not interrupted by some pouty dinner-plate dahlia.

How I would love to wander again in my father's garden. I would insist he allow me entry. Always, the garden was his reprieve, and *his* alone. We were allowed a view only from the sidelines. Early into their marriage, my mother was banished after a weeding mishap when she'd unwittingly plucked out all those pesky baby carrots.

Neither of these gardeners made me heir to their gardening secrets. My father was too impatient, and my grandmother was too shy to impose her knowledge on a reluctant kid. Noel and I have had to gather our knowledge from books, from talking to other gardeners, and from trial and error. I doubt I'll ever have the confidence my father had to plant a garden straight out of the imagination, but he had learned as a child from his mother, and planting was second nature to him. He gardened the way we dream, and unlike his mother's garden, my father's wasn't entirely necessary for food. It was play rather than work. Excess rather than necessity.

My Father's House

MALCOLM, NEBRASKA, 1992

APRIL. Though their house was dark that night, I could still see—lining the sills of the large west-facing windows of my parents' living room—small rooting pots the size and consistency of paper egg cartons. All were filled with the bedding plants my father planned to set out in his garden as soon as the temperatures were warmer: tomatoes, peppers, zucchini, pumpkin, squash, cucumber, melons. Always a large garden, there would still be plenty of room for tall sunflowers, mums, hollyhocks, and castor beans scattered randomly throughout the rows. The early plants—spinach, peas, onion, lettuce, carrots, radish—were nowhere to be found. No doubt Dad had taken them outside to be set once the ground had been worked.

Through my childhood there were always gardens. In all the houses that marked my father's restless changes, the garden had remained a constant. Dad had been taken into his mother's garden when he was an infant. As a toddler he must have followed her, digging between the rows, putting worms and clods into a galvanized bucket. He'd learned the rhythms of planting and harvesting as organically as he'd learned to walk. But he was an only child, and managing one child in the garden was different than managing four active children, all born a year apart. The garden was the only place my father could find quiet away from our noisy household. And so, in my family, the garden was taboo, something to be

168

admired, the fruits of which were to be enjoyed—but the garden itself a temple and my father its only priest.

That night as I stood in their dark living room, I knew how my father would have looked earlier that April day working the ground, having already rototilled the large space behind their acreage, overlooking a small valley. Having removed his jacket and wearing only his gray sweatshirt, the sleeves pushed back to the middle of his strong forearms, he would have stopped now and then in his labors that afternoon to survey the view, to breathe in the fresh musky smell of the newly turned earth. He would have crumbled the dark soil in his hands, testing by its consistency whether he needed to add peat moss or humus or more of the horse manure he'd just hauled from a neighboring acreage. I think I know how he must have felt, too, as he stood up and glimpsed again the panorama of the Nebraska countryside in early spring. He must have felt a slight thrill of contentment. Just being alive was good.

I'd moved out of my parents' roomy house the previous fall, the three kids and I having stayed with them for the first nine months after I left Ross. During those months I woke before anyone else in the house. Outside on those mornings, no lights appeared anywhere on the horizon. In the middle of the night I often woke to hear coyotes yipping and howling on the hills to the north, and once in the predawn, I saw out my bedroom window a sleek red fox running through the snow.

Behind the house, my father had built pens and an aviary for the exotic birds he raised: quail, Japanese pheasants, and chickens from all over the world, each one more bizarre than the next, all of them with a tendency to preen and carry on like pet poodles, their combs and cockles and feathers like elaborate hairdos, or ruffles, or baubles of jewelry. My father's unlikely favorite was the wild turkey. I watched as on a number of occasions he held and stroked the young tom, whose long scaly neck stretched up so the bird could nibble my father's ear, its sparse feathers barely covering the pink-gray flesh. Dad cooed and clucked, and the tom replied in kind.

Once the tom acquired his full growth, he seemed to fancy himself king of the backyard farm, a delusion furthered by my father's tendency to let him run free. When my mother complained the turkey didn't like her and had actually started to attack her when she left for work each day, Dad was amused, not quite believing her. It wasn't until he watched her leave the house one day, carrying with her a large piece of cardboard she'd fashioned as a shield—slight protection it turned out against the bird's assault as it threw its entire weight against her, its wings battering the air—that he understood what was happening. Dad was shocked by what he saw and wondered later why Mom hadn't insisted he take care of the situation sooner. By the time she returned home from work that night, he'd killed the turkey.

Dad was just as impulsive when later that same autumn, after noticing how a wild male pheasant had been making regular visits to the captive females in the backyard pen, he left the pheasant cage open. Later, he watched with satisfaction from the house as the female pheasants solemnly followed the wild male out of the cage and into the fields. Dad told me they all walked single file over the hill across from the house.

Despite his affection for animals, my father retained the rancher's sensibility about them. If an animal in your keeping was sick or crazy, you killed it. If a strange animal wandered onto your property and you happened to feel it was a threat or a pest, you killed it. So while in the backyard he tenderly nurtured his delicate birds, he would, as he thought occasion demanded, step onto the balcony off the upstairs bedroom—where he kept a rifle—to shoot at a coyote or a rabbit or a stray dog. It was not uncommon to hear a rifle shot in the middle of an otherwise quiet afternoon.

My father had come full circle to this acreage from the ranch where he grew up and worked with his father through my child-hood, a ranch he was determined to leave one way or another, even though he was an only child and his father and mother depended on his help with the cattle and crops. He'd wanted out of ranching, but here he was, planting a garden each year big enough to be called a field and raising exotic birds that required every bit the attention and trouble of livestock. But he was happier, more satisfied in recent years than I'd ever known him to be.

It had been a month since I'd last seen him. Only the week before I'd called to tell him I wanted to come out, that I had the money I owed him and Mom. They'd helped with attorney's fees early in the divorce procedure. He waved aside my repayment. "Don't worry about that right now. We don't expect it."

"No," I insisted. "I've been saving to pay you back. I appreciated your help when I needed it most." He seemed to understand then this was about my establishing my independence, and it'd been no mean trick to save that money with the low-paying job I'd found at a real estate company. He acquiesced, seemed proud of me for having proven myself competent and responsible, something I suspected he'd sometimes doubted.

When I'd come to see him the month before it was to watch him make bread. He was known for his breads, grinding the various grains himself, often concocting his own recipes, some better than others. Every time I saw him, it seemed he had a fresh loaf of bread to share. He collected and improvised upon the recipes of traditional peasant breads from Europe: Swedish limpa bread was my favorite—dark rye with fennel seed, a little sweet. I'd begun to feel that baking bread was a holy thing and, after passively watching him make bread for years, had decided I wanted to take it one step further and try it myself. So we'd worked together that day in early March.

My bread was a failure as I realized that day that bread making was not about recipes, not really even about technique, but about something much more primitive. Baking bread was about listening and feeling deep inside, letting the yeast speak through the dough, kneading the dough to life. I recognized it would take years of working beside my father (as he had beside his mother) to become an expert bread baker, not just an afternoon of listening to his instructions.

I remember my father was a little ill at ease the day I came to bake with him. I was a little uncomfortable too. We'd never been particularly close. The oldest of the four kids, I'd often disagreed with him while I was growing up. Our arguments had started in the early seventies when I, in junior high school, was peripherally caught up with the political issues of the time. He was as adamant in his beliefs as I in mine, and each dinner through those teenage years was a clash of two people entrenched in their own version of the truth. I now understand how miserable it must have been for my three younger siblings and for my mother, but at the time, I was aware only of how awful it was for me, for I either cried through entire meals or was banished to my room. It was understood my father and I didn't know how to talk; we only knew how to argue. The reason we hadn't argued during the past year from our opposing stands on the first Gulf War was because we'd both made an excruciating effort to stay away from such incendiary topics.

In spite of our infamous failure to get along, my father had never let me down when I needed him most. He was always there, whether to take the sliver out of my thumb or to come late at night to pick me up after a ball game. Later, it would be my father I most wanted when there was any sort of real trouble, the person whose comfort I most sought after Gary was killed. We couldn't talk—that went without saying—but I could depend on him no matter what.

When my marriage to Ross crumbled, however, I feared it would be the last straw for my deeply religious father. I feared his tolerance for me would at last be exhausted. But he'd been there again as always, both he and Mom, doing what needed to be done, moving furniture, buying beds, making temporary room in their house for me and the kids.

THE NIGHT I SAW the fledgling plants in the window of my parents' house, I felt like an intruder. I walked into their unlocked house and knew the instant I walked in that was no one was inside. I swallowed hard as I shut the door with a soft click and wandered in the dark house for a while before I found the bedding plants in the living room, balancing their overlarge sprouted leaves and flowers on spindly, white stems that looked subterranean rather than something meant to survive above ground. All the while I ignored the eerie red lights of the various emergency units flashing through the room. Though the windows were closed, I heard men talking outside, the occasional burp of a police radio, vehicles coming and going. When I parked my car earlier, I counted four police cars, an ambulance, two fire trucks, several vehicles with flashing lights temporarily attached to the hood driven by volunteer firemen from the area, and another unmarked car I later learned belonged to the county coroner.

Mom had told me earlier on the phone how she'd arrived home that evening to see smoke coming from the backyard, Dad burning off the old garden, though even then she knew it was nothing quite as innocuous as that, for their new puppy was running distractedly in the yard when she pulled up. The front door was unlocked as she came into the same dark house where I stood now. She must have felt the same emptiness, the same palpable lack of a human presence I now felt. But just to be sure, I know she would have walked through every room, all of them orderly and silent. Strange, though, how she hadn't turned on a single light in her search.

By the time she got to the back patio door, she knew. She knew. The fire meant to burn off the garden had burned down the hill behind the house, low-burning but clearly out of control. Clouds of black smoke from the damp grass billowed into the blue-black sky. She felt her flesh goosepimple as she stepped out the door and pulled her jacket tighter, her high heels scritching on the concrete patio. She walked toward the dark garden. Beneath the acrid smell of smoke, and something else she couldn't quite identify, came the musky smell of damp newly turned earth. And then she saw him. He was lying on his back still holding the handle of his hoe, his glasses thrown back onto his forehead, clearly dead. Later, she told me she'd said out loud, "So, it's all over then?" as though she expected him to answer.

My father adored my mother. It was clear to anyone who knew them he was completely devoted to her. Despite his obvious adoration, he couldn't have been an easy man for her to live with. Prone to fits of rage, he often used her as a scapegoat for what was going wrong in a given situation. For the most part she took it—though never in a cowering sort of way—but now and then she made it clear he'd gone too far. As my mother stood in the damp April dark, her thoughts must have been for herself, how she had few regrets, how she'd loved him well.

The neighbors had already called the fire department about the fire they'd seen burning all evening. At first, they hadn't worried, knowing my father was doing his annual preplanting burn-off. But by 9:00 P.M. the fire seemed to have burned out of control, and they were getting nervous. Shortly after my mother found my father, the emergency vehicles were there. He'd died, they later decided, of a massive heart attack around 4:00 P.M. But when I arrived, the cause of death was still to be determined. County officials had yet to confirm my mother had not, in fact, killed him and tried to destroy the evidence of her crime.

That night the coroner swept inside, lights suddenly flooding the dark house as he looked through the bottles of pills my father had been taking for several years to treat congestive heart failure, which at only fifty-seven had made him a very sick man. The coroner asked my mother questions about her whereabouts. "You were just getting home from work at nine? You work in retail? Can anyone verify your whereabouts?" Was there a moment of doubt in my mother's mind, a wild accumulation of thoughts? Did I murder my husband? Did I wish him dead? Did I cause all this ruckus and somehow not know it? And then just as quickly, the answers. "Yes, I was just coming home from work. My whereabouts can be accounted for."

The fire had added a grotesque element to the night, and the macabre image of my father's burning body had seared its way into my mother's memory. Later she would complain that every time she closed her eyes she saw it.

Five weeks later, mid-May, unusually warm but slightly overcast—one of those bleak Nebraska days where the slate-colored sky seems oppressive and the landscape, even in spring, is ugly and dull—my three siblings and I spent the day helping my mother sort through the years-long accumulation of a man who had loved too many things. A basement, a garage, and a large outbuilding were full of things to be sorted and sold: guns, ammunition, fishing poles, tackle boxes, shell-loading equipment, fish-lure kits, candle-making kits, a pasta maker, a food dehydrator, knitting needles and yarn, incubators for bird eggs, feeding trays, watering bottles, rototiller, table saw, router, drills, numerous tools for both carpentry and car repair, cut glass, antique dishes. The list was long. So much stuff. All of it a testament to my father's diverse and androgynous interests. For if he was a man's man—hunting, fishing, woodworking, and fixing vehicles—he was more than just a man's man: knitting, baking, writing poetry, preaching. Who was he?

In one day, the effects of a complex life had been disposed of. By the end of it, we were all demoralized not so much by the work as the way we had so summarily boxed away our father's life. Hardest for my brothers, I'd noticed. Several times, they had to stop in the middle of a task to reminisce about a certain fishing pole, an outing, a "remember when dad . . ." My sister and I, who didn't have such strong memories associated with specific objects as they did, had noticed through the afternoon as one or the other of them disappeared, surely to cry in private.

BY THE END OF MY first year away from home, when my father left the ministry and continued to sell water softeners for a living, I believe he'd experienced a heartbreak, a disappointment in life so keen he could never fully recover. Although those in the medical profession would most likely dispute it, I felt he'd internalized his failed ministry in the form of the heart condition that would seventeen years later take his life, for not long after he left the ministry at age forty, he required a quintuple bypass surgery. A man in good physical condition who neither smoked nor drank—the doctors had been at a loss as to the cause.

My father was the only man I knew as a child who could cry in public. Mostly he cried when he was touched by something beautiful, and he wasn't afraid to speak of his feelings in a tear-choked voice. And it's that I remember best, how my father could come clean, how he could talk about what he really felt in an era when men were discouraged from such displays of emotion. I think now he valued honesty more than anything.

My father was out of step with his time, off center. It's what makes trying to describe him so difficult. He was a crazy man given to keeping rifles and shotguns and pistols stashed throughout the house. He was a man who loved the birds he raised so much he sat up through the night tending incubating eggs and nursing sick chicks back to health. He was a sensitive, creative man. He was an ignorant backwoods farmer given to get-rich-quick schemes, to shortcuts of all kinds, and he was a man of fervent spiritual faith. Was it these contradictions that had so enraged him? I've spent a lifetime trying to understand him and find myself at this juncture with nothing I can call understanding, only a marveling acceptance of his uniqueness.

If I could ask my father one last thing, I'd ask him the names of things: the trees, the plants, the weeds along the ditches, the flowers, the grain growing in the fields, insects, and birds, which he could identify by their calls. My father had looked closely at the world around him. He'd been given the names of these things by his mother, who'd been given them by her father. I'm tempted to construct a gender symmetry in the passing on of knowledge in my family tree, father to daughter, mother to son.

My father broke the cycle with his children, for none of us knows how to name the natural world as effortlessly as he, and my children are now also ignorant in that most fundamental way. Because of this lack of definition I fear I don't observe as I should, and it feels like a terrible loss. When I see something I don't recognize and can't name, my first impulse is to call my father for the answer, in hopes that I'll hear him say once more "brome-grass, dock, meadowlark, diamond willow, cicada, milo, ragweed, tickweed, thrush, Russian olive, lamb's ear, goldenrod, red-tailed hawk, shrew, barn owl, wolf spider, mourning dove," that I'll hear his voice once more telling me exactly what I'm seeing.

May 2002

ORDINARILY BY NOW we would have already planted annuals in the flowerbeds and started planting the vegetable garden, but this year we were only in May making our first visit to the garden center. Given the extremes of weather in the Great Plains, come spring the congested garden centers attest to our pent-up feelings. I've joked in the past that the weather in Nebraska is beautiful for one week in May and another week in September. In May, Nebraska can be almost perfect. The grass is a vivid green; the trees are starting to leaf out, their leaves a pale, delicate mist of green. Peonies and iris are in bloom. Flowering trees and bushes are everywhere. In the yard of the pink house, the redbud in front bloomed, as did the plum, crabapples, serviceberry, lilac, and sand cherry in the backyard. The bridal wreath spirea spilled across the front porch, their fronds so heavy with blossoms the sprays draped across the lawn as if in exhaustion. The leaves of the grapevine in the back were still pink, clenched tight as babies' fists. On the streets around us bloomed flowering pear, forsythia, magnolia, and weeping cherries. May in Nebraska is a fulsome, riotous time, and in a harsh place such a vivid rebirth is heady and intoxicating.

As we drove to the country house, we saw the countryside come alive, too. Calves, colts, and donkey foals ran in the fields and corrals we passed. The air was clear and fresh, the big sky a pale blue peculiar to spring on the Plains. Fat clouds floated serenely above.

The grass on the hills was lush and green, the dark, furrowed fields ready for new planting.

Despite our work at the country house, we couldn't imagine not planting a garden at the pink house. "Nick and Suzi will want basil and tomatoes," I said, and Noel agreed. It was a simple garden we planted: eggplant, green pepper, basil, and tomatoes, but it felt good and right to see a garden growing there still. Nor could we imagine not having produce for ourselves come late summer, so Noel took precious time from work on the house to help me plant the garden at the country house.

When we first took possession of the country place in late October, we looked around and wondered about the best place for the vegetable garden. We discovered at that time that the soil near the house was a heavy clay we knew would need serious amending. Ingrid's former garden plots were so infested with saplings and bigger trees that they didn't seem promising. Not for the first years anyway.

I found the ideal place for the vegetable garden by accident. Behind the pole barn was the foundation of what had once been the original barn. Ingrid had told us the barn had burned down long before she arrived. Weeds had infested what I guessed had been the barn's dirt floor. With the kids' help, I set out one day to clear those weeds by hand because the mower couldn't get over the foundation footings. To our surprise, the weeds came up easily, and we quickly realized the earth in this area was a mixture of old manure and ash. Unfortunately, it had also been used as a dump, and after removing the weeds, we spent hours clearing the area of rusty wire, old metal, broken bottles, and other debris.

"I think I may have found a place for the garden," I told Noel when I went up to the house later that afternoon.

"Oh, yeah?" he said. He was in the middle of hanging doors. Two sawhorses stood in the living room, where he was cutting the trim boards and routing out the holes for doorknobs.

"Where the old barn was. The soil is really soft and dark."

"Let me finish this, and I'll come take a look at it," he said, con-
centrating as he measured a piece of trim board.

Later, as he knelt and ran the dirt through his fingers, he agreed
with me. "My only concern," he said, "is that old oil may have been
dumped in this area." I didn't respond, not quite sure what to say
to this news. He shrugged then. "I don't see evidence of it though,
so we might as well give it a try." He smiled at me ruefully. "I guess
if we all get sick, we'll know not to plant here again."

NOEL WAS PRESSED to finish hanging and trimming out the
doors, racing against the scheduled arrival of the painters. His father's identical twin brother, Lloyd, was a professional painter, and
he and Floyd found time in both of their schedules to come help
us paint all the interior walls, doors, and trim the first of June. Although they were both retired, they seemed to be busier than ever,
and Lloyd still had a full schedule of painting jobs lined up every
month. Floyd frequently flew from southern California to Denver
to help Lloyd, and this project was a barter Floyd had made for
working on future jobs with Lloyd pro bono. They often did this,
trading work on one of their sons' places since Lloyd, like Floyd,
had two grown sons.

While Noel finished hanging the doors, I continued to pack the
house and tended the two gardens. I did my annual thinning of
perennials at the pink house. This year I took cuttings of day lilies, sedum, raspberries, hostas, iris, columbine, and peonies to the
country house, where half the vegetable garden had been set aside
for a plant nursery. We hoped enough of these transplants would
take so we could harvest them later as we began to landscape
around the house and in the backyard. We knew not everything
would survive, but as I placed each young plant in the soil of the

country house, I wanted to believe some would thrive, evidence of our gardening efforts at the pink house, a literal transplanting of our previous labor, the offspring of years of work.

I wanted to pack the house in earnest, but we'd recently hired a new editor at University of Nebraska Press. She and her husband would be coming to Lincoln in the middle of June to look for a house to rent and the editor-in-chief had asked if they could stay with us. He also wanted me to host a party in their honor during their stay so they could get acquainted with the Press staff. What could I say? Noel said I should have said no, but for some reason I couldn't, and I suspect in part it was because I wanted to entertain one last time in the pink house before leaving. We'd hosted many get-togethers through the years, and I sensed one of the changes in the country house would be fewer parties.

The sun porch upstairs became the box room. I also hid boxes under beds upstairs and in the attic. I packed everything that wouldn't be missed from the main floor and the basement bedroom and bath where our guests would be staying. Noel, meanwhile, could hardly stand to be at work during those days, watching the clock until he could leave for the house. He worried he wouldn't have all the doors hung and trimmed before the painters came. The days were growing longer, and he stayed at the country house later each night, every precious hour seeming to slip by.

Our decision to line one wall of each downstairs bedroom at the country house with closets and to build a large closet in the entryway meant that seventeen six-panel doors had to be hung. Painstaking work. Trim around all of those was to be permanent, while the trim around the windows would be provisional, since we would replace those windows once we'd passed the inspection and locked into our permanent loan. Painting the trim around the windows would be rudimentary. One coat. No primer.

BY THE MIDDLE of the month, the backyard at the pink house was stunning. I moved the patio furniture out of storage. We'd started landscaping the backyard at the pink house only five years earlier, after we added on to the kitchen. We'd built the patio only four years before, and the slate walk a year later. The yews and lilacs along the walk and against the iron fence, the Boston ivy on the arbor, and the serviceberry, dogwoods, barberry, weigela, and euonymus in the berm had all reached enough maturity to indicate clearly our intentions. It was bittersweet to see the result of so much planning and to know we were leaving it. In fact, as of the first of the month we were no longer the owners of the pink house but renters instead.

By the end of May, we were ready to install the water softener and purification system in the new house. Once we decided on the system we wanted, we assumed the process of actually buying the unit would be relatively quick, but the salesman from Ernie's store wanted to earn the sale. As he geared up for his sales pitch at our kitchen table one night, Noel and I exchanged a quick glance and silently decided it would be a pity to say prematurely that he didn't need to convince us when he so clearly felt he did. He had stories to tell, and we saw it was important for him to tell them. So, as he tested the water from the well at the country house and announced we had a serious iron problem—"two parts iron, but no nitrates"—he also needed to tell us about the two little blonde girls he'd met whose hair had turned red because of the iron in their water. There were numerous digressions, including the details of his annual trip to Cancún.

Part of doing this sort of project, we reminded ourselves once again, was building in time for conversation. It was rare to simply do business. Talking—storytelling—was an important part of getting things done.

Another encounter this month was less entertaining. Things

started out well with the countertop folks, but they didn't end well. The shop had come highly recommended, and after talking to them, we understood why. At this family-owned operation, the woman ran the office efficiently, and her husband, a jovial and clearly talented workman, made us feel we'd come to the right place. Unfortunately, it wasn't the owner who actually did our countertop, and whoever they sent in his place did a terrible job. It took Noel only seconds when he went to check on the work to see it had been done poorly: the backsplash wasn't complete; the counter over the space for the dishwasher hadn't been reinforced; the cooktop hadn't been cut out—the template instead thrown on the floor—and the face of the countertop in the corner had been badly cut and glued. None of the joints had been caulked.

Since this was work Noel could do himself, he was furious. It was substandard craftsmanship we were being asked to pay for, and he obviously couldn't overlook it. He undoubtedly overreacted the next day when he went to complain, but it felt like a betrayal, given our earlier good treatment. He confronted the woman in the front office and told me later with regret that he'd said to that nice woman, "Is this how you do business? Because if it is, I'm going into the countertop business and putting you out of work."

That evening, when the owner himself came out to look at the botched job, he admitted ruefully that he would have been angry too. "My wife was in tears after you came in," he said to Noel once he'd corrected the work. "But she'll understand why you were so mad when I tell her what happened. I don't blame you for it."

I walked through the kitchen after the countertops were finished and ran my hand along the surface. I stood in front of the window where the sink would eventually be installed and looked across the property. After the long winter, all those months of doubting, the hopefulness of spring was infectious, and I could almost see my life in this house.

Christ Temple Mission

LINCOLN, NEBRASKA, 1984–1989

HE TOLD ME HIS NAME was Skip, and he looked like a skipper with his well-trimmed white beard and his lean body. I met him when he interrupted a Sunday school class I had no business teaching. I remember I had a guitar that day and we'd been singing a song when he came to stand in the balcony of the sanctuary where our class met.

"Don't let me interrupt," he said, after the song ended and everyone turned to look at him.

"You're not interrupting," I said. "Join us."

And he did. He lingered after the kids had left to go to the church basement where final announcements were made before the end of Sunday school. After that, I saw him now and then on Sunday mornings when he dropped by my classroom, but mostly I saw Skip on the streets where I eventually understood he lived. I took to calling him Skip, the Street Shaman, to myself.

I liked to go to church early during those years and sit alone in the cavernous sanctuary while the lights were still dim. I didn't think of the church as the house of God so much as a place of quiet shelter. I could hear Sister Connie in the basement on those mornings setting up the offering trays and the communion trays. I was glad not to be completely alone, for I've always found an empty church slightly creepy.

I'd been to Sister Connie's house once. She kept an old parrot in her living room. We ate fried chicken together on chairs in front of the silent TV. She told me how when she was young she'd been married to a military man and how while they were stationed in France, he'd tried to kill her one night, held a pistol to her head. Afterward she threatened him with a kettle of boiling water. He must have believed she was capable of pouring it on him because he left her then. She was once a beautiful woman. I could still see that as she told me her story.

I went to church early to kneel alone at the altar rail where the elders knelt to pray with those who came forward after services. I didn't want to talk to anyone about my struggles, but I needed a mercy seat, and on Sunday mornings this was where I found it. I didn't pray at those times. Prayer seemed to have left me; instead, I practiced a distracted meditation, some attempt to empty my thoughts into the quiet.

This morning, Meredith, a troubled young woman from the halfway house down the street, had joined me in the sanctuary. I watched as she slipped into a pew and lay down. Now and then in the quiet I heard her humming to herself. On the wall I faced as I knelt were the portraits of the church's founder and his wife, Daddy Mac and Mother Margaret.

Daddy Mac died before I joined the church, and everyone assured me I would have loved him, that the church now was nothing like it once had been when he was its pastor. Now and then they told me he would have liked me—the highest of praise. I liked to take things to Mother Margaret, pies or fruit, just so I could stop by and sit in her spotless kitchen and hear her talk about when she and Daddy Mac were first married—wild kids.

Mother Margaret had a habit of shifting her ill-fitting dentures with her tongue. They clicked together as she talked. When he was young, before he became Daddy Mac, he'd been a drummer, and when his band wasn't playing, he and Margaret danced "like tomorrow wasn't coming." I could picture it easily as she talked, how they would have spun together on the sanded floors to the sounds of big band swing. But, she always reminded me, those had been "sinful, godless" times; they hadn't known any better then. Later, they experienced a spiritual awakening and were "sanctified," a term I didn't quite understand. What it meant, she explained, was that they renounced sin completely, vowed to live a pure life—no tobacco, no alcohol, no dancing, no cards. They refused unwholesomeness. I didn't say it, but I couldn't see how the dancing I'd imagined was unwholesome.

Following their conversion, Daddy Mac went to the African Methodist Episcopalian seminary, where he studied to be a minister. He hadn't liked the racial politics of the seminary, though, and once he graduated, decided God was colorblind and the church should be too. He wanted a church like a bouquet of flowers, a variety of believers to praise Jesus together, which is how Christ Temple Mission was started and how from the beginning one of its purposes was integration.

When Daddy Mac died of a heart attack, I knew without her saying it that a big part of Mother Margaret had died too. It was only her shadow there playing the organ on Sunday mornings, her body so small Brother Frank had to build a special lift on the pedals so her feet would reach.

AS I STOOD UP from the altar this morning, Meredith stood up from the pew where she'd been lying and came to the front of the church toward me. She was holding a hymnal, her thumb marking a page.

"Play this for me while I sing," she said and thrust the book at me.

I took the hymnal from her and noted the song, "Battle Hymn

of the Republic." People would be arriving soon, but I decided one verse wouldn't hurt as I went to the piano. Hating to disrupt the quiet of the sanctuary, I softly played an introduction. I was unprepared for the bellowing off-key voice that filled the sanctuary. Meredith huffed and shouted the words with no regard to rhythm or tune. By the end of the verse, even though early comers had arrived, she motioned for me to go on, and unaccountably I complied. I was very embarrassed by the spectacle she was making of us, but I played until the end of the verse anyway. Afterward, I stood up from the piano bench and ignored her impatient gesture that I should keep playing.

Later, before services began, Meredith, who had disappeared into the bathroom after her performance, approached me again where I was seated in a pew. She had smeared her mouth with a garish red lipstick, outlined her eyes in thick black rings. On her open palm she held out to me her cosmetics. A gesture of thanks? Some new affection she felt for me? I shook my head no and watched as she went to the back of the church. where, instead of sitting down, she paced through the entire service.

MY FRIEND TONI had decided to start a choir. The church hierarchy resisted: we already had two choirs, an adult choir and a children's choir, but Toni had argued that the adult choir attracted only the elderly members and sang only hymns, while the children's choir sang only children's songs, which left nothing for those in between.

The young adults from the church enthusiastically supported Toni's effort, and from its first meeting the Gospel Workshop Choir was a success. Dr. Dolores played the piano in her own unique boogie-woogie style. Darrell played the bass guitar, and Jeffrey, the drums. Although Toni was not a musician and admittedly could only "sort of sing," she found recordings of the songs she wanted us to perform. We listened. The instrumentalists quickly worked out the chord progressions while the vocal harmonies came together section by section. Toni transcribed the lyrics for us. Now and then if Toni was able to find sheet music for the song she wanted us to perform, I'd be asked to play the piano. They all marveled that I could read music, whereas I felt like a charlatan for not being able, like the other musicians in the church, to play by ear.

When Nita, the petite woman in the front row I barely noticed most Sundays, stepped forward to sing her first solo, I felt a shock. I'd never been in the presence of a voice like hers, a voice so powerful and electric it filled the cavernous sanctuary not only with sound but with what seemed like light. I, for the first and only time in my life, felt moved to tears by the human voice. I later learned Nita was all but illiterate, her life in constant upheaval, but when she sang, she controlled everyone in the room.

I SAW SKIP NOW and then downtown. I liked to buy him a cup of coffee or take a walk with him. I understood he was mentally ill, but I was intrigued by the quirky lucidity of his illness. The way he saw the world challenged all my deepest assumptions; I felt slightly off kilter after talking to him. Not surprisingly, Skip was the most unsettling of all my acquaintances. He scared me a little sometimes, and yet I continued to seek out conversations with him.

One day I invited him to eat with me at a Chinese restaurant. We sat in a booth by the window overlooking 14th Street with our Styrofoam plates of garlic chicken and sweet and sour pork.

"Women shouldn't get tied down before they come completely into their own sexuality," he said with a slightly full mouth. He'd never said such a thing to me before. I hadn't told him anything about my family: my very religious husband who taught at the

university, my three children whom he wouldn't allow to go to
Christ Temple Mission with me. It was no small thing for a fundamentalist Christian woman to attend a church other than her
husband's. I felt as though I was getting away with something to
be going to Christ Temple Mission on my own.

Skip looked at me intensely that day, and I stopped eating, wondered what he was thinking. His gaze suggested he knew everything, and I had a strong urge to confess, but I didn't. He seemed
agitated, irritable. I sensed he was angry with me, though it wasn't
clear why. He told me his story then. He'd been a cop in Chicago.
For thirteen years he'd loved a married woman. They'd met when
he was nineteen and she was twenty. During the years of their af-
fair she promised many times to leave her husband. In the course
of those years she gave birth to three children, all of whom she
claimed were her husband's. One day, and Skip couldn't say what
happened on that day, he suddenly understood she was never going to leave her husband. On that very day, he said, he left his job,
hopped a train for New York, and in the thirty-five years since had
never had a home. I looked deeply into his blue, blue eyes, something I hadn't done before. I believed what he'd told me, and I was
tempted to make him a prophet, to see the story as a warning, but
I wasn't certain how to interpret it.

OTHER PEOPLE TRAVELED. My friends all left; they moved to the
coasts, to Chicago. They sent postcards from South Africa, Mali,
Bali, Caracas, Morocco. I never looked at the atlas or the globe to
see where these places were. I wasn't interested in their specific
locations. I was interested only in their place in my imagination. I
conjured these travels, but even in my daydreams I knew I understood little of the experiences described in the postcards. In spite
of that, I pretended what I saw was enough. I imagined smells that

hadn't been described and conversations that hadn't been alluded to. What I couldn't imagine was the freedom to come and go.

Maybe the same desire for dislocation that led others to travel was what compelled me to seek out Christ Temple Mission. I analyzed my motives. Was I exoticizing these people? There could be no doubt of our difference. On my first visit I sat in the back row of the church. I'd never felt so invisible in my life, and I better understood why people of color have so often referred to white people as ghosts. I felt ghostly, insubstantial, insignificant—so liberated. I hadn't realized how parched I felt, but the singing and talking and dancing and clapping were like life-giving water. So unlike myself, I wanted to lift my hands. My eyes were wide, my mouth hung open, and I took in everything.

For the first six months no one knew my name. They guardedly nodded at me. Though the church was integrated—a handful of Native Americans, a few whites, a couple of Asians, rich, poor, educated, homeless—it was mostly African American. The black ministerial staff set the tone for the church. Even at that time, I didn't regard the reticence of the church members as rudeness. Besides, I was tired of the "friendliness" of the suburban white churches. When after six months the church members finally greeted me by name, their greeting meant something. It didn't mean I was one of them—I never kidded myself about that—but it meant they'd taken notice, that maybe I'd stick around awhile.

I didn't plan to stay the five years I did. I remember once standing in the church basement during a potluck, surrounded by the comforting smells of green beans and ham, fried chicken and cornbread, recalling the potlucks in the basement of the church in Litchfield I'd attended as a child. I remembered the expansive sense of generosity and affection I'd sometimes felt as a child for that place and those people. That's how I felt that day in the basement of Christ Temple Mission, and even then in the midst of all that warmth and goodwill was the certain sense I was only passing through. Everything during those five years was painfully self-conscious. Still, though I thought and analyzed with a sort of frenzy, letting nothing simply be, I rarely indulged in such nostalgia in the midst of the present. Toni's husband, Dennis, interrupted me that day, handed me an empty plate. "Get in line, Homegirl."

My husband, Ross, attended church functions with me occasionally. When he was there, I noticed a change in the church members. He had a certain formal polite bearing that made them in turn deferential. I wanted to laugh when I saw them act that way, but they intended no parody. I knew them, though, and they were none of the things they presented to my husband. When he was around, they seemed slightly disapproving of me, and although it appeared he approved of my decision to attend a church other than his, they were puzzled as to why I wasn't behaving as I should. I was happiest when Ross wasn't around.

It seemed everyone at Christ Temple Mission deferred to my husband except one friend who told me once, "There's nothing there. He's empty." And somehow hearing it out loud like that caused me to attend—my whole life to attend—and it began the end I'd felt coming but hadn't wanted to acknowledge. "You're going to need a good hard hat," my friend went on to say. When I looked confused, he answered, as though he'd read my palm and seen it all laid out clearly before me, "to protect you from all the shit that's going to come down when you go."

I OFTEN CHOSE TO SIT near the back of the church during services. The sunlight streamed in slanting rays through the stained glass windows. Sometimes one of Toni's daughters came to snuggle in my lap, her hair caught in a handful of bright-colored barrettes. I sang along and clapped and swayed with the congregation;

I listened to the sermon, not sure what to expect since Daddy Mac's replacement, his nephew Kendall, was not exactly orthodox in his Christian beliefs.

Through the years, Kendall and his wife had taken in seventy-seven foster children in addition to their own eight. He talked to me sometimes about what he was reading. He had a library full of books—not books on Christian theology as you'd expect, but rather books by spiritualists: Edgar Cayce, Annie Besant, and Carlos Castaneda. He believed in the kabbalah, numerology, astral travel, reincarnation, theosophy, anything occult. For the most part, he kept his views out of the pulpit, but sometimes he said something like, "We've had other lives," or "There are worlds beyond this one." If the congregation had been given to booing, they would have booed on those occasions; their disapproval was palpable.

During Sunday school, if my high school students were late or didn't show, Kendall sometimes pulled his heavy body laboriously up the steep narrow stairs to my classroom in the balcony. I heard him coming, his breathing ragged and winded; he had to sit for a minute in a too-small wooden chair to try to catch his breath. Then he told me stories. He was, I eventually realized, trying to convert me to his occult beliefs. I sensed Kendall had chosen to talk to me because he saw I also no longer believed. He saw this in me long before I did. Intellectually, I'd lost my faith, but emotionally I was still invested in the church.

ON A HOT SUMMER DAY I ran into Skip outside the bookstore on campus. We sat together on a bench out front. He wanted to talk about the Christian belief in an apocalyptic time of trouble and the belief among many conservative Christians that true believers will be raptured, or caught up to heaven. Skip's beard was a bit shabbier than it had been when I first met him. His white hair was greasy. Clearly, the years spent on the streets in this cold Nebraska city had been hard on him. "Everyone believes," he said that day, "that in the Rapture it's the good people who will be going up, but what if being left behind is good? What if the ones left behind are the ones who get rewarded?"

I STOOD ON THE second row of the choir, third from the end in the alto section. Toni had assigned our places, and I questioned why she'd put me next to Sister B. Sister B. had no sense of rhythm. She clapped out of sequence, swayed in a random way, frequently bumping me with her bony hip, as she was given to ecstatic reveries in which she threw her hands up and prayed in a fevered whisper, "Thank you, Jesus," then brought her hands down, clasped them together and leaned forward into a bow, her head shaking as though saying no to something. Although I loved Sister B., I had enough trouble remembering the words to the songs and keeping to the right rhythm without her going off beside me, but beside Sister B. I remained.

When young Raeffe Woods died, his parents, Dr. and Mrs. Edgar Woods, asked the Gospel Workshop Choir to sing. The funeral was on a Saturday afternoon, a warm day in April. The outside doors to the church were left open, and the usually dim sanctuary was lit with a rich sepia light; the women in their hats, the men in their suits, the church interior with its oak floors slanting toward the front, and its oak pews, unchanged since it was built in the late twenties, all made me feel like a time traveler. Five preachers had come from out of town to join three of the ministers from Christ Temple Mission. All eight ministers sat together on the stage in front of the choir, each of them assured his or her chance behind the pulpit, or the "bull pit," as they called it. I shortly realized this was a competition, an oral performance before an appreciative audience.

By the end of that very long afternoon, the congregation had been worked into a state of frenzy. The women fanned themselves with paper fans tucked behind the hymnals in every pew rack. Sister B. was perhaps the happiest and most exhausted of all. She'd twisted and shouted and danced and raised her hands and Amened until I was tired for her. We were all spent but sated too.

Then Sister Karen began to sing. The congregation joined her. Dr. D. found the key on the piano, Jeffrey the rhythm on the drums, and then Darrell came in on the bass guitar. The choir sang until the last member of the congregation filed out of the building and into the bright sun.

At Christ Temple Mission I had a distance from church ritual and church rhetoric I'd lacked most of my life. I was neither the minister's daughter, nor the dutiful wife. I could simply be me. In the midst of that distance, I realized this: I genuinely loved these people; I didn't care who they were or what they'd done; I simply loved them. Over the course of those years, sitting in the back row at Christ Temple Mission, deliberately disengaged, I saw the rituals and the rhetoric finally as only that. "I get it," I thought. "We're just people trying to make sense of our lives, trying to make sense of a world too big to ever understand. We're just people needing something to get us through from one day to the next." And I forgave myself, and my past, and I forgave my future as I felt it shift before me.

THE LAST TIME I SAW SKIP was in a thrift store downtown. He smiled at me as our eyes met across the store. His blue eyes weren't angry, and I wanted to think he was prescient somehow and knew that since we last met, I'd left my husband and had fought to keep my children and won in court. He told me he knew he was sick with cancer, and I saw he was thin, his skin dry and yellow. "Have you been to a doctor, Skip?"

"A doctor?" He was impatient with me. "What will they do? I'll tell you what they'll do. They'll lock me in the hospital, poke me, cut me to pieces, make me miserable, and then I'll die anyway." He shook his head still frowning, and then, as if to change the subject, he smiled at me. "I didn't see you last time I was down there to Christ Temple Mission."

"I don't go there anymore."

"Why's that?"

"I guess I thought and thought until I thought my way right out of the church."

Skip laughed. "Is that so?" Before he left, he said, "I'll still be seeing you around town then."

"We'll get a cup of coffee next time. Really talk." Maybe I was thinking as I said it that I'd finally tell him everything, confess my lost faith, my broken marriage.

Only a few weeks later, a friend of mine who worked with a local agency on aging asked me if I knew Skip had died. I hadn't heard. "They put him in Lancaster Manor," she said. "Someone found him collapsed on the street. He died the very next day."

June 2002

"YOU'RE LIKE A CAT with her tailing swishing," said my friend Roìsìn. We were drinking tea at the kitchen table in the pink house, where we'd sat together so many times before her move to Minneapolis. She made her pronouncement in her wonderful Irish way after hearing my still wildly fluctuating feelings about the impending move. And she was exactly right. I was twitchy, alert to every little change, anxious with indecision. Like others, though, Roìsìn thought we were nuts to be leaving the pink house, and her vehemence surprised me. After all, she was a great risk taker, not overly attached to places or things.

Roìsìn's visit coincided with that of the painters. Floyd and Lloyd had driven out together from Denver the first week of June. As usual when they're together, they were dressed alike when they arrived. The first day on the job they were also dressed alike in paint whites: white shirts, white paint overalls, and white painter's caps. They spent their lunch hours at the café in the nearby village of Cortland, where they marveled over the low prices for their daily strawberry malts. By the end of the week, they knew all the waitresses by name.

Floyd and Lloyd are the only identical twins I know well, but I assume the competitiveness I see in their relationship is typical. In addition to being very close, they tend to be hypercritical of one another. Every difference between them is magnified. One has a slightly bigger waist size, one has a slightly higher correction in

his glasses, one has slightly worse hearing. Along with the competition, though, is a unity like nothing else I've ever witnessed.
Once, when they thought I was going to be critical about an area
they hadn't finished painting—an erroneous assumption on their
part since I was so grateful for their work I couldn't imagine being
critical of it in any way—Lloyd immediately moved from another
part of the room where he'd been working to stand beside Floyd.
They stood side by side as if prepared to do battle, both talking to
me at once, hastily explaining the supposed oversight. I laughed at
their antics, seeing clearly a strategy they must have developed as
little boys, talking fast, talking gibberish even, trying to make the
accuser laugh, anything to deflect blame.

THE FIRES STARTED early in 2002, and by June it seemed all the
West was in flames. Lloyd called home to Denver every night to
talk to his wife about the progress of the fires in Colorado. They
were getting close enough to Denver to cause concern among
those living in the farthermost suburbs. One of Lloyd's sons and
his family lived in those mountain areas, and Lloyd was anxious
about the safety of their property. The air above Denver was dark
with smoke, he told us after hanging up the phone one night. I
was cleaning up the kitchen, and I listened, entranced by Colorado
place names, as Lloyd and Noel talked about the progress of those
fires, their voices blending together like poetry.

As the twins painted inside, Noel worked outside hanging exterior light fixtures and hooking up the doorbell, before moving
back inside to cut out the many recessed lights in the kitchen and
living room, keeping barely one step ahead of the painters. The
job pushed Floyd and Lloyd harder than they'd anticipated. Lloyd's
jobs in Denver were almost always in huge houses. When he returned to Denver he would paint a thirteen-thousand-square-foot

house, and he'd just finished painting an eight-thousand-square-foot house before coming to Nebraska. He'd clearly underestimated how long it would take to paint a measly eighteen hundred square feet. Also, Lloyd was responsible for painting all the trim and the doors, and he pointed out that seventeen six-panel doors were as many as he usually painted in much larger houses.

When they finished, though, the rooms looked fresh and clean, and at long last it was time for the floors to be finished. Carl B. had made the successful bid and spent a good while looking over the house. Despite the rough appearance of the wood floors, Carl assured us they'd sand out beautifully. We figured if anyone knew, it was Carl. He had an ax to grind that day about all the new development going on in Lincoln. "Those big, overpriced houses," he said. "What are those people going to do if the market drops out? How are they going to get rid of those houses?" We were standing in the room we'd designated as Bronwyn's room, arguably the sweetest room in the house with its two east-facing windows looking across wooded meadows to the red barn, and its south-facing window framing one of the elm trees along the drive. Carl B. shook his head and looked around the room. "This is going to be a real nice place here."

The four days the sanders were working felt like a holiday for Noel, and he felt a little guilty for—as he put it—puttering. That week he hung the provisional siding on the new entryway and painted it, did some work cleaning up around the exterior of the house, mulching and laying paving stones for a temporary walk; and at last, he built two sets of provisional stairs, one off the front door and another off the new entryway to the south side of the house. He scolded himself after he was finished for not having built those stairs sooner. It would have made all those trips in and out of the house with debris, tools, framing boards, and Sheetrock so much easier.

THE DAY THE FLOORS were to be finished, we drove out together
to take a look at them. A bit tentative about what we'd find—for
this step, more than any other, would complete the house—we
peeked in through the windows first. "They look good," Noel said,
and I agreed. As soon as we stepped inside, we were greeted by the
sharp, warm smell of the polyurethane finish. The air still smelled
of sawdust too. Inside the sun shone through the windows across
the fir flooring. The floors were a rich red gold. Any doubts we may
have had about how the damaged areas might sand out were put
to rest. The damage only added character. We walked on sock feet
through every room, seeing at last the home we'd held so long in
our imaginations. It was modest and simple. There was nothing
remarkable in any of its features, no fancy elements of any kind,
but we had worked hard to achieve that simplicity, and it was no
accident. We were like little kids in our new house exploring as if
we didn't already know every inch of it.

At last, after all these months, the house seemed as though it
might be finished on time. It had gone from construction zone to
almost finished house in a matter of two weeks, and after so long
working without seeing dramatic results, these last touches, paint
and finished floors, confirmed the rightness of Noel's confidence
in what the house could be.

Seeing the end this close didn't mean we could relax, though,
and Noel pushed himself even harder now to meet the final re-
quirements for the inspection. He finished hanging light fixtures
and fans, screwed on electrical plates, trimmed out around the
pantry and oven, and finished, with our new neighbor Mark's
help, the plumbing in both bathrooms; he then put on doorknobs
and removed all the brass hinges that had come with the doors
and replaced them with brushed nickel. Meanwhile, I scraped and

primed the inside stairs and primed and painted all the new trim around the pantry and built-in oven.

At the pink house, I had initially planned to sell the nicer antiques on my own and to have a garage sale for the rest, but when one of my colleagues at the Press, who sells antiques part-time, suggested I have an auction, it seemed like a good solution. She even recommended a father/son team with an excellent reputation, especially among antique dealers.

When Mr. F. came to look at what we wanted to sell, he admitted it would be a small auction. His suggestion of combining our things with those of two other clients and splitting the advertising costs three ways seemed reasonable to me. He explained they generally took fifteen percent of the proceeds unless it was clear the auction wouldn't cover their expenses in which case they would have to charge for labor. Because he couldn't schedule the auction for the third weekend in July as we'd hoped, we had to settle for the second Saturday in July, thereby committing ourselves to moving two weeks earlier than we'd planned. I arranged for the moving van and lined up a few friends to help that day. The auctioneer assured us they would dispose of everything that didn't sell during the sale, so I cheerfully packed, knowing the house would be emptied after the sale, leaving me plenty of time to return to clean before Nick and Suzi took possession at the end of the month.

The one piece of furniture we couldn't decide about was the baby grand piano. It had always fit perfectly into one corner of the large living room of the pink house, but I worried now it might dominate the living/dining room of the country house. The truth was, I'd been so busy in the past few years I rarely played anymore. It felt extravagant and vain to take it with us. Noel, however, disagreed. "You need to take the piano with you." His sentimental attachment was not a complete surprise. He knew well how all my life I'd had a piano in every house where I lived.

We were still debating, though, at the time Mr. F. came. "The baby grand?" he asked that day while he compiled his list of items to advertise. I looked at the piano and hesitated. "I'm not sure about that yet. I'll let you know before you place the ad."

Earlier in the month, while we were also still debating about the stair railing, not quite seeing a traditional wooden banister on that short steep stair and along the stairwell on the second floor, I had proposed a metal railing. Perhaps I'd been inspired by the cattle fences I'd been seeing regularly in my drive to the new house, but a horizontal metal railing seemed a better fit with the aesthetics of the house than any other option. Noel agreed with me. He felt he could do the welding necessary to build the railing. The only problem was he'd have to find a portable welder since it would require onsite welding and measuring. For several days we brainstormed about how to borrow or rent a welder, until I finally suggested we just hire Bruce, the only welder we knew, to do the job.

"I don't know about Bruce," Noel said, and his misgivings were well founded. Bruce did things in his own way and his own time. He was an excellent welder, though, and had worked on numerous projects we admired in Lincoln's Haymarket district. Despite his reservations that Bruce would be capable of meeting our strict deadlines, Noel agreed to talk to him.

Bruce and his old dog Barney drove out to the country house in the ancient jeep he used to haul his welder. A friend was visiting from Texas, and we all sat down together at the picnic table in the front yard to discuss the railing. I sensed my friend's dubiousness about our entrusting anything to Bruce, and I couldn't blame her.

Bruce wore his gray hair in a haphazard shaggy mullet he'd obviously cut himself. He was skinny and strong, like a rangy coyote. His clothes and his person were always grimy with the residue of his work. He was a good guy but an odd one, and in conversation he digressed frequently. He lived in a little house in Lincoln filled with things he'd scavenged from dumpsters through the years. The accumulation had by this time moved well beyond the house and into his yard and garage. His jeep appeared to be held together with duct tape and baling wire.

While we talked, a family of woodpeckers flew back and forth to the nest they'd built in a dead limb of one of the big elms bordering the driveway, and we all frequently interrupted our conversation to watch in fascination as the birds came and went.

Bruce looked over the project we proposed and told us he could do it easily in three days. We'd been hopeful he might have some design suggestions based on the space, but he established early on in our conversation he was a craftsman only, not a designer. He could do whatever we asked him to, but he couldn't come up with a design. He'd brought along not only a portfolio of his previous work but also catalogs that might give us some ideas. I was surprised at such a level of professionalism from Bruce.

Barney, his dog, stayed at our feet while we talked, his tail thumping slowly if anyone looked his direction. He liked people, but he didn't like our dog, Finnegan, who wanted to play with him. Throughout our meeting, Finnegan kept approaching Barney eagerly, and each time Barney responded by baring his old yellow teeth and growling a deep, menacing growl.

The day after the meeting with Bruce, Noel measured and drew up a simple "cattle gate" design for both the stair rail going up and the two rails at the top, which he transferred in detail to graph paper.

When he delivered the plan, Bruce was delighted and confirmed once more he could finish the job in three days. Between the two of them they decided Bruce would start the project over the long Fourth of July weekend, completing it the day before we were scheduled to move in.

By the end of the month, I'd finally concluded with Noel that we should plan to move the piano. We measured the southeast corner of the living room and found it would fit there fine. I was still concerned that the piano would overwhelm the space, but Noel was right. I would have missed having it.

I'd begged for piano lessons as a very little girl and had started playing at the age of five. Always rebellious, I rarely had a piano teacher I liked. I loved playing but resisted practicing the scales and finger-strengthening exercises they all recommended. Despite this, I worked hard to learn the music to accompany various singing groups and, as a young girl, had made the piano an important part of my life.

I'd found the 1923 baby grand at a thrift store in Omaha. It had obviously been cared for and played through its long life. Still in tune when I found it, all the original ivory keys were in perfect condition, which had prompted me to ask how it came to be at the thrift store. I was told it had been donated by an older woman who'd remarried, to a man who already owned a baby grand. All her children also owned baby grands, and no one in the family had a need for this one. I never regretted the purchase, and I was happy now that Noel had prevailed against my pragmatism and persuaded me to move it to the country house.

THE HOUSE I MOST OFTEN dream about is not a house where I lived but is instead the house where my mother grew up. When I dream about the rooms of that old farmhouse, I sometimes add entire wings, rooms emptying into other rooms. I'm always happy after I wake from those dreams.

The yard of my maternal grandfather's house was filled with mature trees: oaks, cottonwoods, elms, and sycamores so plentiful the air was pungent with their sickly sweet smell when the round seed balls were ripe. A creek ran through the property, and the corrals for the cattle were tucked away down the hill from the house in the woods near the creek. My grandfather kept the red barn and all the outbuildings painted and tidy.

My mother's parents had been happy. I hear this in the stories she tells, of a family laughing together, a mother who, with no provocation, would dance an Irish jig in the middle of the kitchen, a father who adored this mother so full of life. My mother's father had been among the youngest of twelve children in an unhappy family of German immigrants. The entire family lived in fear of the patriarch, who expected his wife and his seven sons to work the farm while he came and went, keeping his "fancy ladies" in Omaha. My grandfather vowed when he was a boy that if he ever had a wife and children he would treat them all with love and respect.

I never knew my grandmother. I'm told she laughed too loudly, something my mother grew to love but which embarrassed her as a child. Her mother died when my mother was twenty-five. My grandfather was lost without her. Left with a twelve-year-old son to raise and three grown daughters with families of their own to care for, Grandpa closed off most of the rooms of the big farmhouse, but he and my Uncle Larry continued to farm together, forming a new sort of family.

My mother openly adored her father, calling him Daddy always. She told me once he'd never criticized her; instead, when she made something or did well in school, he'd greet each effort with pleasure and surprise, "Did you do that?"

As kids, we never liked to visit him. It wasn't that we didn't like Grandpa, but his house seemed lonely all shut up that way. He used only the large L-shaped kitchen, the bathroom, and one bedroom adjoining the kitchen. We were bored by the confinement of his truncated house, especially in winter.

In the evening, he watched an old black-and-white television encased in a blonde cabinet that sat across from his lounge chair. We always arrived at the end of the day, after he'd shaved and bathed from his work outside. On those nights, he smelled of Burma Shave, his long white hair freshly slicked back from his bath. He looked vulnerable without his cap and wore, winter or summer during our visits, only Key overalls (always the herring-bone, never the blue denim), leaving the top buttons on the sides unopened. I occasionally glimpsed, against my wishes, a bit of the top part of his briefs and his exposed white sides. His large arms and belly were white and soft like a fish belly while his ham-sized hands were ruddy and rough. He had a large head and heavy features, a thick mouth, a big nose, a prominent brow, and long, fleshy-lobed ears. He liked to tease us, but he didn't know how to make us feel at home.

At Christmastime, my Uncle Larry and his wife, Kay, came the week before to open up the house. They aired the rooms, scrubbed and cleaned so that on Christmas Eve when we pulled into the sycamore-lined drive, we saw the huge farmhouse with its wrap-around porch all lit up, where it was usually dark. It looked like a mansion those Christmas Eve nights, like Brigadoon, something mysterious appearing only once a year for a short, magical time. The cars of my aunts and uncles filled the yard, and cousins came running to greet us as we arrived.

I often conjure an image of my mother, something I've fabri-cated from a story she once told me about how she learned to play the piano. When she was a child, her desire to learn to play was so strong that despite the lack of a piano and no money to buy one, she drew a keyboard on cardboard that she laid out on the family's kitchen table at night and taught herself how to read the notes. I see her there in an island of light cast by the kerosene lamp, head bent in concentration, looking up quickly to the music book, then down again to her keyboard, playing a silent song, imagining it sounds beautiful. I picture her with scratched legs, wearing a print cotton dress, homemade of course, her hair in pigtails the way I've seen it in photographs.

In the dim light, desire burns on her face as she plays her silent piano. It is a metaphor for her life. Determination in the grimmest of circumstances, putting the best possible face on what is unconscionable. An exquisite denial. She's one step ahead of anyone who might try to discourage her; what she can't find a way to change, she'll revise and reinterpret until it's okay. And remarkably, because of her belief, it often becomes okay.

She was born in Nebraska in the middle of the Depression. Before her father and mother bought the farm where she spent most of her childhood, they lived as migrant workers, staying with relatives in La Grande, Oregon, where her father picked peas through the spring, and then traveling back across the country in their makeshift camper to Hyannis, Nebraska, where her uncle owned a pool hall. The family lived above the pool hall while her father worked nights in the bar below.

My mother owns a piano now, a little Baldwin upright with soft white keys and a pecan finish. She doesn't play when we're around, though I often see a hymnal out, and I know she must play when she's home alone. She lives with her new husband in a house she built after Dad died. I imagine she plays the piano now with the same intense concentration she had when playing her paper keyboard, the notes not quite as beautiful as those she'd once imagined. She must look up at the hymnal, then down again quickly, hesitating slightly before depressing the keys, never having learned to play without looking, not trusting herself to have the right notes beneath her fingers. But, in spite of this, the chords come out whole, the tune finds its shape and holds. In spite of those small mistakes, it is a recognizable song.

The Doll House on Everett Street

LINCOLN, NEBRASKA, 1991–1992

THE IDEA OF SCATTERING grass seed on top of the snow after an early March blizzard had seemed laughable when my aunt advised it, but I wasn't laughing that Saturday morning in the cold March sun as I stood in my snow-filled yard throwing grass seed. I would have done anything to try to get grass to grow on the muddy front lawn of the house where I was living with my kids. It was a rental house, which in theory I shouldn't have cared about, but I did care. I cared because this was where I was living and because I was tired of the kids tracking mud into the house. I'd put up with it for the seven months we'd been living there, but as spring grew near, I wanted grass.

Every Saturday morning, without exception, I cleaned the house thoroughly. I kept it spotless, more so than any other house where I'd lived. It wouldn't be a stretch to interpret this frantic clean-ing as a projection. Cleaning seemed at the time the only thing in my life over which I felt any control. Almost everything else was out of my hands. For sixteen months I'd been in a vicious custody battle fighting for the kids—now ages six, eight, and ten—that had spawned some new outrage each week for either me or them. My private journals had been subpoenaed; former fundamentalist friends had been called to testify against me; the children had been questioned in secrecy by lawyers and a psychiatrist; and through it all my ex-husband had maintained he was only doing it out of love for me. He was, he told me, concerned that I didn't know what I was doing. He was prepared to go as far as necessary to save me from myself. He was convinced "the devil had gotten hold of me."

My new job, as the director of a writing center in the university's athletic department, was a part-time venture that required me to work four evenings a week, leaving the kids with a babysitter. I'd gotten the call from the academic wing of the athletic department out of the blue. The woman doing the hiring remembered me from an earlier encounter. "We need someone to set up a Writing Center to work with high-risk athletes," she told me that day on the phone. She went on, "We need someone to organize a physical space, write curriculum, hire and train a staff of twelve." As she spoke, my mind raced. This sounded like a big undertaking. Then she added, "We need everything up and running by the beginning of the second semester." Two weeks from the date of her call. They were mad; it was impossible. "I'll take it," I said.

Later, an acquaintance, hearing about the terms of the job asked, "Who would take a job like that?" and I answered, "A single mother of three making five dollars an hour." In other words, someone desperate. Someone exactly like me. And I did what they wanted. By mid-January the center was in operation, fully staffed, with a curriculum in place. In March, as I scattered that grass seed on the snow, I was just finishing a handbook for tutors. Part of my ongoing sense of desperation, though, was that I had no clue what to do with my future, no certainties about how I would support the kids. The job in the athletic department was volatile, and I knew it couldn't last. I was still in graduate school.

Noel, whom I'd met the year before, was the one bright spot in my life, the one source of comfort. Ironically, in my severely pared-down life at the time, my relationship with him was the one thing I felt was a luxury. My nerves were raw, my reserves depleted. What I did not need in my life was one more problem. I was tensed for him to say the one thoughtless, unsupportive thing that would lead me to walk away. It hadn't happened yet, and I was beginning to trust that maybe it wouldn't happen at all, that things could work out between us. I was traveling then with overwhelming burdens, daily confronted with all the problems inherent to poverty and single motherhood. I'd become fiercely pragmatic, willing to jettison anything I didn't need to carry.

My friend Theresa had been the one who found the rental house for me. I called it the doll house because it was a diminutive two-story, on a quiet street near Antelope Park. The house was surrounded by old trees and well-tended homes. Although the house was small, I had insisted on moving my piano. It sat in the living room like a giant, crouching to fit in a gnome's house, leaving space in that room for only a couple of chairs and an end table. I took great comfort from having the piano there, and on those weekends when the kids were with their father, I played for hours as if to soothe myself.

The fact that I needed to be renting this house was one of the many ways I'd come to regret taking my ex-husband at his word. His refusal to leave the family home in the first place was what had forced the kids and me to move into my parents' house initially. At the end of the summer he'd deliberately broken his promise to move out of the house before school started, leaving fewer than two weeks to find a place for me and the kids in the school district before classes began. As long as we were still contesting custody, the marriage couldn't be dissolved; the children were considered "property" by the courts.

This meant, though, that I was still legally part owner of the house where my ex-husband lived. In the fall, fed up before I moved into the house on Everett Street, I made detailed lists of items we needed from each room of the family home. I hired a moving van, gathered boxes and newspapers for packing, assembled a group of friends and family, and on a Saturday morning in September, after first making sure the kids were safely out of the way, descended on the house to move the things I'd left the year before.

Ross was shocked. He hadn't thought I was capable of this. As each item passed out of the house, he stood sentry at the front door, arms folded across his chest. "That's contested," he said of every bed, dresser, or box of dishes." The movers shrugged. "Talk to the judge," they would say. "I'm surprised at you," he said to each of them in turn. "I'm disappointed you could do this to me." Most of them pushed past him, ignoring him. Finally, though, my friend Barb said, "I'm not doing this *to* you. I'm doing it to help the kids."

That day, for the first time since the custody battle began, I felt as though I was finally taking charge of my life.

BY MID-MARCH the snow had melted in the front yard, and every day as I came and went, I looked to see if the impossible had happened and the grass seed had germinated. So far each morning I saw only mud and more mud. At about this time the high school girl I'd hired to watch the kids at night while I worked at the writing center had to quit, and I was left in a lurch. I hired another neighborhood girl. She was younger than the previous babysitter, and I had serious reservations; but her parents were nearby, and she assured me she'd call them if there was a problem.

Each morning as I made breakfast for the kids before school, I asked about the previous evening. Now, near the end of March, unlike their usual bland assurances, the kids were uncharacteristically quiet. Finally Bronwyn said, "Everything was fine after the police left." While the older two shushed her, my heart seized. "What happened?" I said, feigning a calm I didn't feel. Leif and Jordan pressured Bronwyn to be quiet, but she went on to tell me how on

Leif's dare she and Jordan had run out into the street without their clothes on. The babysitter hadn't been aware of it, and a concerned neighbor, not knowing me or where I was, called the police. "So this is what we've come to," I thought as I sat at the breakfast table that morning. "My children are running naked in the street."

BRONWYN, IT SEEMED, was often the odd one out. The year before, the kids had been taken into judge's chambers during one of our court appearances. They'd been accompanied only by the lawyers for both sides, and they'd been sworn to secrecy. They told me about it later, and I sensed their fear in breaking the judge's orders that they were not to tell their parents about what had happened. That evening a year earlier, Leif and Jordan were angry with then five-year-old Bronwyn, the same way they were angry with her now as they told me what happened in the judge's chambers. "The judge told us we had to choose," Jordan finally told me that night, as she looked at Bronwyn accusingly. "But Bronwyn wouldn't choose."

"What do you mean?" I said.

"The judge said we had to choose. You or Dad, but Bronwyn kept saying, 'both.' No matter what the judge said, she wouldn't choose."

The kids and I were alone that night in my parents' house when I heard how something big, and official, and terribly wrong in its disregard for the delicacy of the human psyche had been pressed into the minds of my children in a way I couldn't then, will never, comprehend. I felt I'd lost all control. All my work of raising them well—feeding them healthy food, reading to them, bathing them. and getting them to bed on time, making certain they got to the doctor, to the dentist, to school—seemed undone, not merely by a careless gesture but by a systematic denial and disregard of everything except one side winning and another side losing, no matter what the collateral damage to children. I remember sitting silently a few minutes that night while I thought about what I had just learned.

Finally, I said to the kids, "No matter what anyone told you, you were right to tell me about this. And, Bronwyn, it's all right that you didn't choose. Whoever asked you to do that was wrong. No matter who it was, they were wrong. That would be like asking me to choose between the three of you. It isn't possible." I looked at Leif and Jordan then, who I knew had chosen. I could see the guilt and confusion gathering in their faces. "And you two, don't worry about what you said. It's all right. Everything is all right."

But it wasn't all right, and it hadn't been all right. In the months since then, they'd been acting out in their own ways, and this episode with the girls the night before was only one symptom of their anger and self-loathing. I knew we'd have to work for years—not to undo this damage, it couldn't be undone—to somehow fold it into our lives in a way that worked for us and not against us. I didn't scold the girls that morning in March. I didn't punish them. I sensed they were watching me, wondering, testing. "You both know better than that," I said. "I'm disappointed." And that was it. All behavior had become relative to the great affront of their present situation. All systems had failed them. Their parents, the judicial system, the church. They'd become cynics, my children. They were devastated. We were on new turf, way beyond the usual mother/child negotiations. What in the end would save them all was their sense of humor and their great capacity for loving and forgiving.

THE JUDGE, fed up with how slowly the custody fight was going, scolded the lawyers on both sides for their failure to bring the case to a close in a suitable time. At last we were scheduled for a final court date at the end of March. After all those months of waiting, the court decided quickly to grant me full custody. That was the end of the court's part of the story and the beginning of the long road toward healing.

I was thinking about these things a week later, in April, a newly divorced woman, when out of habit I scrutinized the mud in the front yard. I saw there what I'd come to believe wasn't possible, tiny shoots of grass, so frail and thin I could barely see them. Once seen, though, they were everywhere. Now that I really looked, I could see the yard was covered with new grass.

What I didn't yet know on that April day was that six months later I'd marry Noel and we'd buy a wreck of a house we'd rebuild together and paint pink one day. I didn't yet know and couldn't have dreamed then how I'd rebuild my life as well. I didn't yet know how I would move far away from the indecision, the desperation, the doubt and fear of that time I lived in the doll house. I didn't yet know how my children would grow up confident and kind, how they would find ways to turn the pain of the past into strength, and humor, and creativity. How could I possibly have known any of that as I knelt in the muddy yard of my rental house smiling over that new grass? And yet it was all there in that single act of faith, throwing grass seed on snow.

July 2002

THE GOOD THING about a drought is that the grass doesn't grow and you don't have to mow. That's the only good thing. By July, we'd had no rain for a month. Temperatures soared above 100 degrees. We kept both gardens watered and tried to keep the lawn at the pink house watered, but despite our efforts, by the time we left on the sixth of the month, the yard at the pink house looked rough.

After almost six weeks without rain, nonirrigated fields of corn across the state were past any hope of recovery. In the western half of Nebraska, the grass had died before reseeding, forcing many ranchers to start selling their herds simply because they lacked feed for them. The governor declared a state of emergency, and state economists predicted more than a billion dollars in lost revenue in Nebraska due to the drought.

As Noel and I drove daily past fields of stunted, stressed corn when the plants should have been putting on tassels, we were all too aware of the reality of these reports. From his vantage point in the grain industry, Noel predicted little or no harvest that autumn. The state budget shortfalls endemic across the country were further exacerbated in Nebraska by the drought. Dramatic budget cuts were being considered, with the university asked to bear what seemed, to many in my circle, too great a burden in those reductions.

TRACY, FROM THE GRAIN ELEVATOR, came the night before our move to help Noel and me load Leif and Jordan's things and move them into their apartment. Both the kids had to be out of town that evening, so we arranged furniture, made their beds, and stocked the fridge and the cupboards. I felt happy as we left their apartment knowing they'd be in a safe place surrounded by familiar things.

That night as we prepared for bed, I went through my nighttime ritual of checking door locks and turning out lights, all with the awareness it would be the last night in my beloved pink house. As I moved from room to room, I compared the house as it now was with the house we'd first encountered almost ten years earlier. After I turned off the kitchen light, I stood for a few minutes looking out the large kitchen windows into the backyard at the old maple tree shading most of the yard, the little vegetable garden, the arbor where I'd spent so many happy hours reading, the patio where we'd eaten as a family and with friends. I'd been very happy in this house. It was the place where I learned to trust again, to love again, to hope again for the future. It wasn't only the house that had been transformed in the decade we'd lived there; I had been transformed as well. That night, I silently honored this history for a few minutes before finally going up to bed.

Already by 9:00 A.M. the next morning it was ninety degrees and very humid. I'd carried all the boxes to be moved to the main floor so no one helping us would have to climb stairs, but it was of little benefit as the temperatures continued to rise by the hour. Shortly after noon the temperature had already reached 104 degrees.

I was so busy that day, so determined that things go well, and so oppressed by the heat, I felt almost no emotion as we emptied the house into the truck. Despite the heat, the move went smoothly with an efficient crew of six—two of Noel's band mates (Larry and John), my brother Tad and his wife Diane, Noel and me. We made the move from the pink house to the country house in three hours total.

After the movers had eaten lunch and left, I sorted boxes and arranged furniture, startled now and then by the view out the window. So this is where I live now, I thought each time. The furniture we'd brought with us seemed to fit well with the dimensions of the rooms, including the piano, which sat perfectly now in the southeast corner of the living room, not at all dominating the space as I had worried it might.

As night fell, even with the windows closed and the air-conditioner running, we felt the deep quiet of the surrounding countryside. The darkness was almost complete: no street lights, no car lights. At 10:00, after I'd made my nighttime rounds in the new house, we were still a little giddy at the strangeness of finding ourselves in a new house, and none of us felt ready for sleep. Bronwyn and Finnegan joined Noel and me in our bedroom, and together we watched the evening news, while Bronwyn made us laugh as she clowned with Finnegan. She loved her new room upstairs, and she was excited by the adventure of the move.

We were still watching the news when we heard the first crack of thunder. At the same instant, lightning struck close by, and a strong gust of wind hit the house. The storm came up that quickly with no warning even from the local news program we'd been watching. The quiet night was suddenly filled with the noise of wind and thunder. It sounded like a freight train running through the house. Finnegan, who hated thunder, cowered among all of us on the bed. Out the bedroom windows we watched an amazing lightning show. A flash of lightning close by knocked out the electricity. Then it was Bronwyn's turn to cower. Understandably, she didn't want to go upstairs to her room alone in the dark, and there was no way we could find a flashlight or candles among our packed boxes, so Noel walked her and Finnegan through the pitch black house to her room.

Only then did the rain begin to fall, the first rain in six weeks. It was too late for the corn standing dead in the fields. Too late for the dormant grass in our lawn. But it came as a relief from the oppressive heat and the humidity, and I welcomed it, allowing myself to see it as a good omen. I was reminded that night how almost ten years before when, after Noel and I were married on the lawn of my parents' house, a sudden, brief, rainstorm swept through and left in its wake a double rainbow. I wanted to trust now, as then, that this drought-ending downpour symbolized good fortune.

When I woke the next morning, the world felt washed clean by the storm, and for the first time since we'd made the decision to buy the country house, my doubts about the move had also been washed away. For months I'd hoped for an epiphany, some burst of understanding, but now at the end I experienced instead only a feeling of simple well-being.

As if to affirm my sense of contentment in the new house, among the pieces to arrive in the first mail delivery forwarded to us later that week were two letters with good news for me: one alerting me that an essay I'd published the previous year would be reprinted in the Pushcart Prize volume and the other a letter from the Rona Jaffe Foundation announcing I was a recipient of one of the Foundation's annual prizes for women writers.

BEFORE THE MOVE, as I'd been taking the more delicate things by car to the country house, I'd seen no evidence that Bruce was working on the stair railing. Noel had seen him only one day in late June when Bruce had come out to take measurements, but since then, he'd seen no sign of him either. Our calls to Bruce went unanswered. When we'd moved our things in on the sixth, it was clear nothing had been done on the railing, and Noel and I both felt ourselves begin to panic.

We'd definitely have to have a stair railing in place if we were to pass the inspection in two weeks, and I could see Noel was already thinking of ways to slap together a rudimentary wood railing in case Bruce didn't follow through. We were disgusted with him, though, and Noel reminded me about his earlier reservations, for it was I who had wanted to believe Bruce could do the work he promised. I'd perhaps been overly impressed by that portfolio of his.

Noel's irate phone messages finally prompted Bruce to begin work on the stair railings, but even after he started, we weren't reassured, as every day that first week we were in the house, he arrived casually at 3:30 in the afternoon, puttered for several hours, drank a few beers, ate dinner with us, and lingered until 9:30 or 10:00. I'd taken some time off work and wanted to settle into the new house in peace, but unfortunately, the fiasco with Bruce meant I had a guest every day and evening, and a not very charming one at that. Barney came along with Bruce, and he and Finn squabbled every day. I found myself identifying with poor, old Barney.

It was apparent that at this rate Bruce wouldn't finish the railing before the inspection scheduled for the fifteenth. Even after he finished the railing, it would still need to be painted and screwed into place, and I would have to finish painting all the trim around the stairs and the stair risers. We understood the inspector wouldn't care about the old siding on the outside of the house or the old windows. He wouldn't notice the provisional trim or siding either, but every raw surface had to be painted. All lights, outlets, and plumbing had to work. And a stair railing had to be in place.

Noel finally grew so irritated with Bruce, he started calling him at home early each morning, strongly urging him to get on the job, reminding him once more we needed this inspection before we could lock into our permanent loan. Whereas before this, Bruce's eccentricities had seemed benign, they now seemed like serious personality afflictions, and Noel wasn't sympathetic. He confronted Bruce one afternoon after Bruce continued to argue with him about finishing the job.

"You said you could meet the deadline, Bruce."

Bruce immediately grew defensive. "It doesn't help me to have you pressuring me like this."

"Pressuring you? You didn't even start the job by the time you'd promised you'd finish it. It's been almost a week since the deadline, and you're a long way from done."

Again Bruce had an excuse, "I've been working to clean up my own yard, man." He explained how a neighbor had reported him for all the junk in his backyard. The city had issued a citation, and he'd been given a month to clean it up.

"I don't care about your yard, Bruce," Noel said. "I'm sorry, but I don't. You need to make this job a priority. I'm depending on you, and it's too late for me to do anything else. I'm not going to let you screw up this inspection. You hear me?" Somehow, yes, Bruce did seem to hear. It may have been the murderous rage he saw in Noel's eyes. He told me later, "Noel really scared me. I thought he was actually going to hit me."

"He's got a lot riding on this, Bruce," I said. "He's exhausted. He's worked for eight-and-a-half months straight without a break, and he can't let it fail now because of this. He just can't."

Bruce nodded. "I was being optimistic when I bid the job," he admitted. "I really didn't think I could finish it as fast as I said I could."

"You shouldn't have done that. You weren't listening to us very well," I said.

After that, Bruce seemed genuinely contrite, and he was at the house early every morning, taking few breaks and no longer staying for dinner each night. Despite the rough beginning, three days later, when he finally finished the railings, he and Noel parted on good terms, and we sat down together for a picnic dinner in celebration.

As a testament to his new commitment to the project, it was Bruce who called me at 7:00 A.M. the next morning to warn me about the severe storm moving our way. The railings, he told me, would rust if they got wet. "You should get them moved inside or at least covered," he said.

Noel was already at work forty minutes away, and after several futile attempts I knew I wouldn't be able to move the heavy metal railings by myself. All our tarps were in the truck with Noel. I spent an hour improvising a solution, trying to wrap the railings with plastic garbage bags and masking tape, working futilely as the wind howled around me. I knew if it poured rain, my feeble attempts wouldn't make any difference. The new railings would rust.

Through that day, I continued to watch anxiously out the windows as trees leaned in the wind and black clouds roiled and massed in the west. I couldn't quite believe it when, by evening, after all the ominous buildup, the storm still hadn't materialized.

Later, as Noel and I spray-painted the railings, the sky continued to rumble menacingly. The wind raged. "Wouldn't you know it," I said as I helped Noel lift one of the heavy railings that would line the stairwell upstairs onto the sawhorses. "No rain all summer, and now when we need it to be dry, it's threatening rain."

Noel shook the spray can and looked closely at the metal. He dusted off a speck of something. "We've been lucky on this project," he said distractedly as he began to lightly apply a coat of paint. And as if he were a prophet, we were spared rain.

The next evening Rick and Cathy, who had returned to Nebraska from New York for a summer visit, came out to dinner and to see the finished house. Noel had doubted I could help him move the heavy awkward railings into place without scraping the walls, so Rick helped him move them that night. As the last piece was bolted into place, the house finally and completely came together. The metal railing was exactly the right addition to the space, and at long last we were ready for the inspection two days later.

GIVEN THE MONTHS of work, the sacrifice of time and money, the inspection was inevitably a letdown. To the inspector, this was just another house, clearly one still in progress, merely a small part of the inspector's day. He was one of those middle-aged, graying men of average height and weight, who makes absolutely no impression. And since he made no effort to interact, I remember nothing distinctive about him. He was at the house for a total of fifteen minutes. I timed him. I was being childish, hoping for something more, eager for a word of praise like the gold star on my second-grade spelling test, and although we easily passed the inspection, I had wanted more closure, a more celebratory feeling in its wake. Still, it felt good to call Kelly at Security Federal to schedule our closing date for July 27th.

"The rates are really good right now," he said on the phone. "But they're going down every day. I'm going to lock you in at today's rate. If it goes lower, we'll adjust before you come."

After the auction, Jordan and I returned to the pink house to clean. We were glib as we started out that day, thinking we'd be in and out in a couple of hours. Instead, we were shocked to find not only had the auctioneers failed as promised to cart away the things that didn't sell, but they'd also failed to clean up the garbage generated during the sale. My sewing machine, which hadn't sold, had been left in the backyard and was now covered with bird droppings. The things in the attics of both the house and the garage clearly hadn't even been put on the auction. Jordan and I wandered through those dreary rooms dreading, in the still oppressive heat, the job of dragging furniture and boxes out of the attics and having to dispose of everything we'd believed would be discarded after the sale.

The windows had been shut for two weeks without the air-conditioner running, so the hundred-degree-plus air was unbearably hot and stale. The walls looked badly scuffed now that the furniture and wall hangings were gone. The lawn had been trampled by the visitors at the auction and nothing watered in the weeks since, so the plants in the yard all drooped and had begun to turn brown. That day, the pink house looked so diminished, so devoid of any spirit or life I wondered how I'd ever loved it so much. It was just an empty house. Nothing special at all. I felt sad at my own delusions.

I was reminded of a story one of my former sisters-in-law told about the difference in the letters she'd received from me and my former mother-in-law during a trip we took to Mexico together. While my mother-in-law's letters were full of disgust over what she saw: the dead donkey in the road, the mangy dogs, flies everywhere, the stench of uncollected garbage, the crowded buses, the pollution of Mexico City, I wrote glowingly about walks on the beach, coconut drinks, bags of fresh tangerines, mountain passes, the glories of Mexico City. It wasn't that I hadn't noticed the things my mother-in-law had seen, I simply wanted to see the beautiful and the exotic more. Suddenly, confronted with this empty, lifeless house I'd so loved, I wondered if I'd done the same thing with my whole life. A grand denial. It was a dispiriting way to leave the pink house. As Jordan and I worked together in grim silence, I felt betrayed both by false promises and by my own deluded nature.

The day after Jordan and I had cleaned, Noel went to pack up his shop in the basement and the workshop of the garage, which we'd made off-limits for the sale. After he spent a day trimming hedges, mowing, watering, and weeding, he assured me the yard looked better than it had when I'd seen it. Everything was as ready as we could make it for Nick and Suzi.

When later in the week we received the check and the itemized list from the auctioneer, the amount was staggeringly low, in good part because they'd charged more than forty percent of the take for their labor: they claimed it had taken six people three hours to move sale things onto the lawn. The heat had been oppressive the day of the sale—106 degrees, even worse than the day of our move—and I knew they'd also been hosting the same day another auction nearby, this one an entire three-story house. Given the low turnout and the unenthusiastic auctioneer, I perhaps shouldn't have been surprised that the selling prices were horribly low, but we were charged for the entire advertising bill, making it clear that without explanation the other two clients' things hadn't been included in the sale as promised.

Neither Noel nor I had seen any advertisements for the sale, and Noel wondered aloud now where they'd advertised, "At the City Mission?" A few of the vintage toys had sold well, as had the antique oak bedroom set, but otherwise we were shocked by the low winning bids on many of the other good quality antiques: $100 for a large Empire sideboard; $200 for our 1920s blue velvet couch and chair in good condition; $250 for a pineapple-leg harvest table and six chairs; $200 for an art deco secretary. It went on and on. I read the itemized list with a physical shock. My skin grew cold, my heart raced. I thought to myself, "This is what it's like to be robbed." I felt as much the fool as if I'd left the door unlocked or my purse hanging on the back of the chair at a restaurant. I'd been complicit with my own loss, and I was humiliated. It was like being conned by a very clever man, and we'd allowed it to happen. *I'd* allowed it to happen, since it was I who had made the arrangements, *I* who had failed to get a contract, his stellar reputation and all. I had been duped and was so embarrassed by the sale I couldn't even talk about it for a week. Characteristically, Noel was furious. But neither my depression nor Noel's anger changed anything.

Afterward, Noel called the auctioneer, but he got only a recording, and of course they didn't return his call. He wanted me to follow up in the coming week, and I should have. I should have called the Better Business Bureau. I should have made a stink. But instead I did nothing. I can't explain why every day I promised myself I'd make the necessary calls and then could never bring myself to do it. Perhaps I already felt we'd spend more time and money fighting than we could hope to recover. After all, it wasn't only the money. It was the thought that pieces we'd valued hadn't been valued by others, and there was no way we could hope to make that right again. For the duration of the house project I'd felt as though I was pushing myself to do things I hadn't wanted to do, and I couldn't seem to face one more act in that vein.

Despite this, in the days and weeks following the move, as I feverishly unpacked boxes and arranged rooms, the house began to feel like home to me. Everything was manageable and convenient. No more going up and down two flights of stairs to do laundry or get the vacuum cleaner. The quiet astonished me. It was a quiet so deep I felt it seeping into my very bones, felt myself relax where I hadn't known I'd been tense. It was the same experience we'd had on vacations; and I better understood our new neighbors, Mark and Linda, once telling us they no longer needed to leave home to get away. We slept soundly at night. Nothing woke us from our dreams.

On the morning of the 27th, we met with Kelly at Security Federal. As he'd suspected, interest rates had dropped even further since we'd called earlier in the month. Not only had we finished the project in time to meet the deadline of the loan, but during a period of uncertainty and economic volatility post-9/11, we were locking in to record low interest rates at the end.

Later that night, we toasted each other in our new kitchen. "If I'd known . . . ," Noel shook his head before going on, "We couldn't have finished this without all the help we got." There was no denying it. We hadn't done it on our own, and we were grateful beyond words to those who had helped. But I knew Noel had overseen the project well: no serious delays, no miscalculations, no major mistakes requiring expensive backtracking. He'd thought through each phase of the project, and we stood together now in a house we'd dreamed into being.

The process of leaving the stability the pink house had represented for me was helping me to see it was all right to make a change. Besides, I thought that night, stability is a state of mind as much as it is a state of being. I was reminded, too, of what I thought I'd known before the move, that home really is the people we love and the traditions we carry on. Sometimes the most obvious truths are the most elusive. I don't take happiness for granted, but I'd learned something about my marriage to Noel through this process. We can make a home anywhere.

That night as I looked to the east, toward the red barn in the meadow now at dusk lit dramatically by the setting sun—the view I'd known I could live with when I first saw the house—I realized such promises are not vague or inconsequential. They're what our lives are made of. Already a bit reclusive, I worried Noel and I might become too isolated in our self-contained world. But earlier that evening as we'd worked in the garden and later cooked dinner together, it came to me how overrated most social engagements are and how good it felt to be safe at home sheltering with someone I loved, tending together to the essential things, the things I still believe are most sacred: books, bread, animals, gardens, good friends, and family. And while I have left my earlier faith, I have retained my belief in its most important tenets: love, forgiveness, mercy. Oh mercy. Always mercy.

"To us." I said as I raised my glass to Noel that night. "To us," he said and met my glass with his.

ACKNOWLEDGMENTS

PARTS OF THIS BOOK first appeared in the following literary journals. "Litany for the Last Days" first appeared in *Prairie Schooner* 76.3 (Fall 2002) and is reprinted with the permission of University of Nebraska Press, copyright 2002 by the University of Nebraska Press. "House of Pain," originally titled "The New Woman Next to Me," is reprinted with thanks to the *Connecticut Review*; "Our Infamous Failure" is reprinted with thanks to the *Clackamas Review*. The essay "Fields of Mercy," which first appeared in *Fourth Genre* and was later reprinted in the Pushcart Prize Volume XXVII, served as the inspiration for telling parts of this story in its present form.

In 2002, with the help of a generous gift from the Rona Jaffe Foundation, I took a month away from my then position as an editor at University of Nebraska Press. In those weeks of focused work, I wrote the chapters that chronicle the month-by-month story of the work we did gutting and rebuilding the country house. It was an unexpected gift, for which I remain deeply grateful.

Much earlier, in the 1990s, I began writing the pieces that would eventually form the intervening backstory that I, at a later point, realized was centered around the various houses where I'd lived. Through that period, members of the No Guilt Writing Guild gave me valuable feedback. Here it is at long last, ladies. With deepest thanks to Liz Ahl, Chauna Craig, Kate Flaherty, Erin Flanagan, Sherrie Flick, Gaynell Gavin, Charlotte Hogg, and Sandy Yannone.

As this book began to assume its current hybrid shape, I was given help and encouragement from many generous and smart people. The book's failures are all my own and its quirks the result of my mischievous mind; however, it's a better book for the attention of Janet Silver, Dawn Marano, Pamela Painter, Jennifer Brice, Elisabeth Chretien, Jim McCoy, Charlotte Wright, Rebecca Marsh, and my children: Leif, Jordan, and Bronwyn.

This book is dedicated in part to all those who helped us renovate the country house. Most are named within the pages of this book, but there are others, unnamed, who lent support, encouragement, time, and tools. Thank you all. We couldn't have done it without you.

Thank you to our neighbors in the country who made us welcome. In addition to Mark and Linda Gentleman, the Behrens brothers, Ken Krueger, and Marian Krueger.

My siblings were the great companions of my childhood and are now adored friends. They were more present in my life than this memoir reflects. No doubt, they would tell some of these stories differently than I have, but I hope I've done justice to our shared past.

I've had the immense good fortune to be Elaine's daughter. Thank you, Mom!

Special thanks to my in-laws, Floyd and Marie Eicher, and especially to Floyd, who was there at every step, helping us to make a home out of rubble.

And finally, thank you to Noel, the love of my life, who built a beautiful house in the country, a house he loved waking up in every morning and loved coming home to every night, and a house he eventually left when my work took me to Boston. After reading this book, I think you'll agree: If that isn't love, I don't know what is.